The 2020 California Consumer Privacy Act (CCPA) Definitive Guide
(2021 Release)

An Applied Solution Using NIST 800-171

Mark A. Russo, CISSP-ISSAP, CISO
Former Chief Information Security Officer (CISO), Department of Education

DEDICATION

This book is dedicated to the cyber-security men and women that protect and defend the Information Systems of this great Nation.

This is also dedicated to my family who has been supportive of my endeavors to plunge into writing as not just a hobby but a calling to make the world a better and safer place.

The 2020 California Consumer Privacy Act (CCPA) Definitive Guide . Mark A. Russo
Copyright © 2021 Cybersentinel LLC. All rights reserved.

Printed in the United States of America.

October 2019:   First Edition-A

Revision History for the First Edition

2019A: First Release-A

2021B: 2nd Release

Good Processes Provide Good Test Artifact Outputs—If there are none, then the process has <u>NO</u> value

Most Extensive Cybersecurity Blog Site

This is the major resource of everything "Cyber."
"The good, the bad, and the ugly of cybersecurity all in one place."

Join us at https://cybersentinel.tech

This free resource is available to everyone interested in the fate and future of cybersecurity in the 21st Century

The 2020 California Consumer Privacy Act (CCPA) Definitive Guide

(2021 Release)

Table of Contents

(Even More) Forward

Governor Jerry Brown signed several amendments to the CCPA in late 2018 having significant impacts for 2019 and 2020. California's legislature gave its Attorney General (AG) additional time to develop implementing rules and has moved the enforcement date to no later than January 2020. It is possible the enforcement date maybe sooner, but unlikely, based upon challenges the AG is facing in executing oversight and compliance efforts for the state of California. This includes the lack of understanding of necessary cybersecurity measures and clear directions on legal enforcement mechanisms; this also includes appropriate notifications, warnings, and punitive actions against businesses and their owners who fail to comply with the CCPA. Companies should be preparing to be compliant by January 1, 2020 and be prepared for enforcement actions by July 1, 2020. This appears to be the latest schedule for CCPA implementation and enforcement, and this guide is specifically designed for the transition in 2020.

One amendment under consideration provides CCPA exemptions for personal data handling with regards to federal laws to include the Gramm-Leach-Bliley Act and Health Insurance Portability and Accountability Act (HIPAA). Health care providers and banking institutions, Senate Bill (S.B.) 1121 explained that the CCPA does not apply to health information subject to federal HIPAA requirements and personal information controlled under Title V of the Gramm-Leach-Bliley Act. Also, the CCPA does not apply to the use of personal information obtained from or transferred to a credit reporting agency according to the Fair Credit Reporting

Act (FCRA). This exemption does not relieve the need for data privacy protection but allows for other cybersecurity protection frameworks that are mandated by the federal government—and in fact, which may be more stringent such as NIST 800-53 or more likely NIST 800-171, revision 1, Protecting Controlled Unclassified Information in Nonfederal Systems and Organizations.

Another amendment adds language specific to fines that could be as much as $7,500 per intentional violation; the definition of "intentional" remains a difficult challenge. It will further add to the implementation of timelines and uncertainty. The California legislature also removed the requirement to notify the state AG within 30 days of filing an action. The AG no longer has the power to unilaterally approve or dismiss the company's initial actions to attempt in good faith CCPA compliance.

*A final amendment notably updates that a consumer has a right to be deleted from a company's databases. This would include company site notifications of changes and adherence to the CCPA, or direct email to consumers who chose for regular notifications of their data. Proper notice disclosures and consumer rights to access, delete, and a notice of the sale of their data will have the right and mechanism afforded by the company to opt-out. Furthermore, companies will be required to have full knowledge and inventory of all personal data they store and process. This most likely will require a **data inventory**[1] being created as part of a company's compliance effort.*

---

[1] See the chapter: *Consider a "Data Inventory" to the System Security Plan (SSP)*

The 2020 Updates

The Current Amendments

Amendments to the California Consumer Privacy Act (CCPA) continue to advance on in the California legislature. There is a September 13, 2019 deadline for the legislature to pass all associated bills and measures required for CCPA implementation. The Senate Appropriations Committee authorized six bills, Assembly Bills: AB 25, AB 846, AB 1564, AB 1146, AB 874, and AB 1355—See below for a more detailed discussion. The bills have been ordered to the Senate floor for consideration without any hearings; *all bills are expected to move to the Governor for signature in late 2019 through early 2020 period*. Two of the bills, AB 874, and AB 1355, will be placed on the Senate's consent calendar because they have not been opposed, and they too are expected to be ratified.

Furthermore, the California Senate Appropriations Committee also voted to advance AB 1202, the data broker amendment. This amendment is not expected to be considered or passed in 2019. This procedural action holds the bill for future consideration and is not expected to be ratified until 2020 or later. Specific reasons for AB 1202 not advancing is because the bill has a significant fiscal impact on the State of California's budget. Additionally, because of the technical nature, members of the legislature to not have the requisite expertise to understand nor implement its provisions; it will require outside subject matter expertise.

2019 CCPA Assembly Bills

- **AB 25: EMPLOYEE EXEMPTION:** Assembly Bill 25 modifies the CCPA it does not cover the collection of personal information from job applicants, employees, business owners, directors, officers, medical staff, or contractors.

    - **PLAIN ENGLISH:** *If the collection of personal data is part of normal operations, the above exemptions allow companies and agencies to collect data as a matter of meeting their everyday needs. However, it does still require that those exempts are still required to adequately protect and secure such data in a secure manner from unauthorized disclosure to those without an explicit need-to-know.*

- **AB 846: LOYALTY PROGRAMS:** Assembly Bill 846 allows businesses to collect personal data, spending patterns, etc., that do not interfere with a company's loyalty or rewards programs.

- PLAIN ENGLISH: *It does not interfere with companies collecting personal data and collecting such data to target advertisements, tailored mailings, etc., to enhance their ability to use that information for its commercial use. (However, it does not preclude companies from selling this information to third-party vendors, data brokers, etc.; expect this law to come under immediate scrutiny by watchdog organizations and the public.)*

- **AB 1564: CONSUMER REQUEST FOR DISCLOSURE METHODS:** Assembly Bill 1564 requires businesses to provide at least two methods for consumers to submit requests for accessing and identifying their personal information. It requires at a minimum a toll-free telephone number. For those businesses that only maintain an online/Web presence, they must provide an email address for submitting CCPA requests.

  - PLAIN ENGLISH: *Consumers will have at least two mechanisms to access their personal data; however, the bill does not provide for responsiveness, completeness, etc., to the consumer. Expect this bill also to be delayed into 2020.*

- **AB 1146: VEHICLE WARRANTIES & RECALLS:** Assembly Bill 1146 exempts vehicle information retained or shared for purposes of a warranty or recall-related vehicle repair be secured.

  - PLAIN ENGLISH: *Unfortunately, CCPA fails to require in-state and out-of-state car warranty and similar databases from the requirement to implement stronger cybersecurity measures. While this bill is not expected to be scrutinized like AB 1564 and 846, respectively, it does pose potential damage to the public by not requiring at least adequate security measures such as those found in NIST 800-171.*

- **AB 874: PUBLICLY AVAILABLE INFORMATION:** Assembly Bill 874 restructures the definition of "publicly available" information. The new definition, as found in AB 874 states that it is lawfully available data or information from federal, state, or local government records. The bill also seeks to amend the definition of "personal information" to exclude "de-identified" (anonymized) or aggregated consumer information.

  - PLAIN ENGLISH: *This is one of the better bills under consideration. It creates a legal basis for information outside these areas, federal, state, or local, as "not publicly available." It creates the basis for a violation of the CCPA where businesses share information among businesses. (This may be accidental but creates a future means for the AG to punish companies in California under the CCPA).*

- **AB 1355: CLARIFYING AMENDMENTS: Assembly Bill 1355** exempts de-identified (anonymized) or aggregated consumer information from the definition of personal information.
  - ○ **PLAIN-ENGLISH:** *It creates a "forcing function" upon businesses to ensure they create policies and procedures to de-identify and aggregate data to demonstrate their due diligence. If a business does not consider how to accomplish this, it may be fined under current provisions of the CCPA.*
  - ○

Placed on Suspense File of the Senate Committee on Appropriations

- **AB 1202: DATA BROKER REGISTRATION: Assembly Bill 1202** requires data brokers to register with the California Attorney General.
  - ○ **PLAIN ENGLISH:** This bill will probably not be considered until late 2020 to 2021 due to the complexities of monitoring and enforcement. The legislature will have to define what it means by a ***data broker***[2] and create an organization within the AG to manage their existence within California.

2020 Top 10 Recommendations

While some of the following recommendations may be more technical in nature, they have been consistent standards for whatever cybersecurity framework used and approved under the current guidance that the California AG is expected to support. It may require further consultation with your on-staff IT personnel, but the intent is to provide established best practices already solidly accepted with the cybersecurity community.

1. **Implement all Security Controls as best as possible.** Whatever the cybersecurity framework used, they all require identifying and implementing security controls within the company or businesses IT environment. Controls are devised to not only address the technical aspects of the control but also, for example, the company's public reputation. Also, be aware that a Plan of Action and Milestones (POAM) is ***entirely acceptable*** if the solution cannot be implemented technologically or financially immediately; let the POAM be "your friend."

2. **"Agility" occurs through "Continuous Monitoring" (ConMon) of the IT Environment.** While no company can monitor every aspect of a threat, either external or internal, it must embrace a continuous monitoring effort. This does not have to be a purely automated review of the

---

[2] Data brokers are typically third-party companies that buy personal data and use it for targeted reasons. This may include product sales, understanding buying patterns, etc., that are not disclosed by the company that had collected the data in the first place.

technical controls, but manual checklists, reviews, and testing afford reasonable efforts to protect IT assets and data.

3. **Understand the Principle of "Adequate or Reasonable Security."** The frameworks are looking for a "good faith' effort that the protections are in place. Companies will initially conduct its own "**self-assessment**" and providing that information to the State or designated agency. This will include documents and artifacts that demonstrate "reasonably" meeting the security controls. *Have you done everything you can do (currently) to ensure the security posture is enough to prevent unauthorized access to the IT network?*

4. **Seek Greater than "Adequate."** While adequate is an acceptable, more significant implementation of controls should be the objective. Always strive for a "fully compliant" solution by using other mitigating controls through a "Defense in Depth" focus.

> When implementing a secure IT environment, the System Owner (SO) [the business owner of the resources] should utilize the "Defense in Depth" principle for cybersecurity protection of corporate or agency sensitive data.
>
> The broader protections in any IT environment are devised around the Defense in Depth (DID) principle, also called "layered defense." It may include, such additional protections to a company or agency's IT assets:
>
> - Physical protection (e.g., security fencing, alarms, badging systems, biometric controls, guards)
> - Perimeter (e.g., firewalls, Intrusion Detection Systems (IDS), Intrusion Prevention Systems[3] (IPS), "Trusted Internet Connections")
> - Data (e.g., Data Loss Prevention (DLP) programs, access controls, auditing)
> - Application/Executables (e.g., **whitelisting** of authorized software, **blacklisting** blocking specified programs).
>
> Technical solutions alone are not guaranteed to fully protect a network from outside threats and certainly will not prevent an insider threat with full rights and accesses to your system. While they afford additional means to slow hackers and nation-state intruders, they are not total solutions. The government, and much of the cybersecurity community, actively support the principle of **Defense in Depth (DID)**.

---

[3] Most IPS include IDS capabilities; the objective is if employed, an IPS will both "detect" and "prevent" the intrusion.

The Principle of Defense in Depth

5. **Be Honest.** This process is only as good as the effort the business truly commits to protecting privacy data. To be successful, rely on your internal and external subject matter experts, resource appropriately, and demand excellence in control implementation. Shortcuts will only result in future weaknesses that make the company susceptible to cyber-attacks.

6. **Mitigate, Mitigate, Mitigate.** Do not rely only on a singular technical solution to meet the control in total. The weakest link in any organization is its people. Look to the People, Process, and Technology (PPT) triad as a holistic approach to a sound defense.

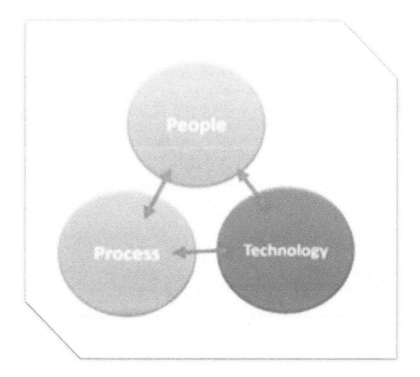

The PPT Model is the recommended guidance for answering many of the controls. While all solutions will not necessarily require a technological answer, consideration of the people (e.g., who? what skill sets? etc.) and process (e.g., notifications to senior management, action workflows, etc.) will meet many of the response requirements. The best responses will typically include the types and kinds of people assigned to oversee the control, the process or procedures that identify the workflow that will ensure that the control is met, and in some cases, the technology that will answer the control in part or in full.

---

7. **The Success of Cybersecurity Rests with the Leadership.** The failure of cybersecurity has been due to the lack of senior leadership involvement in the process. This should be their role in providing direction, seeking current threat updates, and especially resourcing to include trained personnel and dollars for the tools needed to protect the corporate infrastructure.

8. **It is Risk Management and not Risk Elimination.** It is the recognition of the risk (or threat) that is documented and captured as part of a POAM (see above in recommendation #1) that ensures awareness and appropriate responses within the company's IT environment and by its leadership. Avoiding the identification, especially of incomplete control implementation, creates the most significant risk.

9. **The Power of the POAM.** The POAM is not a "sign of weakness." It is an acknowledgment of where problems may arise and helps in planning, resourcing, and focusing effort to future resolution. (Start with IDENTIFY, and continually look to improve the company's internal processes concerning its cybersecurity protections).

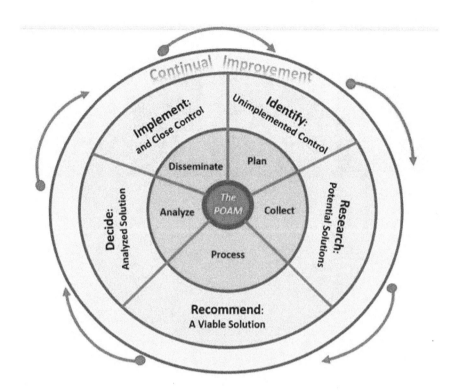

The POAM Lifecycle

10. **When working with the government, keeping it consistent and straightforward works.**
Simplicity is your greatest ally when working with these new processes. Align responses to the controls as described with the selected framework. (Recommend the National Institute of Standards and Technology 800-171 or the National Cybersecurity Framework (NCF) which are free, open-source, and non-proprietary; see other books available from the author at Amazon).

Consider a "Data Inventory" to the System Security Plan (SSP)

In the age of data protection and privacy, is it not imperative we have a Data Inventory? Do companies and agencies know where and who is protecting their vital data? Data that could include privacy information, Intellectual Property (IP), Controlled Unclassified Information, personal health records, etc., need to be known not just for cybersecurity and privacy purposes, but growing State requirements to protect or be FINED laws.

New York and California are expanding such laws. Specifically, current deadlines are fast approaching for California and the California Consumer Protection/Privacy Act (CCPA).

What would have to be part of such an inventory? Here are a few suggested areas that should be added to better tracking data within a company or agency's IT environment.

- Locations of all database repositories (physical locations)
- Is a Cloud Service Provider being used?
- What specific data security protection controls are being used? (NIST, ISO 27001, etc.)
- Is there shared security protection in place?
- Is there an active Service Level Agreement (SLA)?
  - How often is it reviewed?
  - How often monitored?
- Number of current records
- Types of information stored (IP, PII, PHI, etc.)
- Whether the data is encrypted (Data at Rest (DAR) encryption requirements)
  - What product is being used for DAR encryption?
- Privileged Users with elevated privilege access (System Administrators, Database Administrators, etc.)
  - What product(s) are being used to track unauthorized access/use? (Automated audit log reviews)
  - Insider Threat protections and programs

Compliance Requirements for Covered Businesses

To implement the CCPA, it requires several compliance and implementation requirements and includes:

1. **Modification of Disclosures and Websites**—Sections 1798.120(b) and 1798.135(a) of the CCPA requires that informational disclosures be provided to consumers, including the functionality of websites. Companies must regularly update their online privacy policies and California-specific consumers' privacy rights specific to CCPA.
    a. This can be implemented in several ways:
        i. Banners and posts on the main home page.
        ii. "Push-notifications" to consumers who have selected regular notification via email or text messaging.
        iii. A dedicated CCPA Page clearly identified and made available from the company's home page.

2. **Information Requests from Consumers**—Businesses will have 45 days upon receipt of a valid consumer request. Covered businesses are required to disclose and promptly deliver the requested information at no cost to the consumer. Companies will be required to provide requested personal information twice a year. Additional requests will most likely be at a reasonable cost yet to be determined by the California AG's office.

3. **Training and Creation of a "Consumer Response Team"**— A covered business will have to recruit, train, and staff a Consumer Response Team (CRT)[4] to receive consumer requests for access to their data and the state/disposition of that data at the time of the request. This will include a request ticketing system, notifications (both manual and automated) to the consumer, and auditable logs of actions and their status that will likely be assessed by the AG when a violation is reported/investigated.

4. **System Design**—An *implementation program* may include the following:

    a. Policies and procedures that are technologically implemented to comply with the CCPA;

    b. All testing and independent verification and validation activities to include test plans and reports that result from verifying CCPA compliance.

    c. Maintaining a "data inventory" (as described above) as a potential effort to determine types and locations of privacy data, any associated support processes,

---

[4] This is the author's conceptual term, and not currently defined by the State of California specific to CCPA implementation.

databases, and repositories. This will likely include requirements by the company to know the security state of all data held and maintained by a third-party provider to include, but not limited to, a Cloud Service Provider (CSP). This also includes contracts with all suppliers and vendors involved with data collection, maintenance, and care of CCPA-related data and information.

    d. Training and educational activities that include employees and specialized Information technology (IT) personnel responsible for oversight of privacy-related data. This should include all notifications by corporate personnel to an assigned privacy officer/office when a violation has been recognized;

Exemptions for Certain Business Data Collection and Data Transfer Activities

The CCPA has several exemptions specific to data usage. These are the currently defined exemptions for privacy data as defined under the latest 2018 update impacting businesses for 2019:

(i) Publicly available personal information;
(ii) Information used to comply with a consumer's inquiry and direction;
(iii) Information used for a customer transaction such as a sale or return action;
(iv) Sanitized information that is not useable to identify or reconstruct the original customer's identity;
(v) Information needed security purposes, legal review, or for law enforcement investigation.
(vi) Information used for free speech purposes, not in direct violation to CCPA and the US Constitution.

The recent update to Section 1798.145 of the CCPA explains the responsibilities levied by the CCPA on a covered business. It does not restrict the business from:

(i) Complying with state or federal laws;
(ii) Respond to civil, criminal, and administrative actions, investigations, and proceedings;
(iii) Using anonymized (or "de-identified") consumer data that obfuscates the individual and any related personal data fields that could be used to "reverse engineer" the person or persons identity
(iv) Collecting information "if every aspect of the commercial conduct takes place wholly outside of California." In other words, the CCPA only affects companies conducting business and collecting personal data of citizens of the State of California.

Potential Enforcement Actions

For enforcement actions by the AG, the CCPA allows the imposition of penalties for *intentional violations*. Under the CCPA, fines are as flows:

(i) Up to $7,500 per intentional violation
(ii) Alternatively, $2,500 of unintentional breaches if a business fails to cure inadvertent breaches within 30 days of notice of alleged non-compliance.

For enforcement brought by a private plaintiff with regards to data theft or security breaches of Section 1798.150 of the CCPA allows statutory damages from $100 to $750 per incident--or actual costs, whichever is greater. A notice must be provided to a covered business providing them an opportunity to correct the alleged violation. S.B. 1121 removed the authority of the AG to intervene in cases involving a private party based upon the recently approved amendments described at the beginning of this chapter.

Attorney General Rule-Making Authorities

The CCPA allows explicitly any business or third-party to request guidance from the California AG "on how to comply with" the CCPA. Section 1789.185 directs the AG *to promulgate regulations clarifying the requirements of the CCPA*. (This is a significant authority, and as discussed earlier, the AG is struggling with the mechanisms to assess and further enforce the CCPA will likely lead to further delays).

 The Attorney General has until July 1, 2020, to issue implementing regulations.

What is the CCPA?

If you are reading this book, you are most likely seeking a "game plan" to meet the requirements of the California Consumer Privacy Act (CCPA) of 2018. This book is designed to provide clear direction and understanding of how to implement the National Institute of Standards and Technology's (NIST) 800-171 cybersecurity framework. The information is explicitly provided to the CCPA either for a business, agency, or organization that is required to meet this new State Law. The CCPA provides several provisions specific to California residents and the companies that operate within its borders. The CCPA provides California residents the right:

- To know what personal information is being collected about them
- To know whether their personal information is sold or otherwise disclosed and to whom
- To have the right to prevent the sale of their personal information by a business that has collected and stored such data
- To be able to access their personal information and its deletion under specified situations
- To receive an equal quality of service and price when they execute such privacy rights under the CCPA; there will be no discriminatory action for those residents who opt-out of sharing their personal information with a business

Further, this book is designed to explain how to best implement NIST 800-171, revision 1, *Protecting Unclassified Information in Nonfederal Information Systems and Organizations* security controls. It helps the business to effectively meet these controls for the purposes of CCPA compliance.

The CCPA allows the use of NIST 800-171 where there is an absence of a codified standard. It ensures that security policies and practices of the candidate framework meet the intent of the CCPA. These not only include NIST-based frameworks, for example, NIST 800-171 and the National Cybersecurity Framework (NCF), but several internationally-recognized information security frameworks as well. An example would include the Center for Internet Security's (CIS) 20 Critical Security Controls. Adoption of these or equivalent information security frameworks ensure accepted security policies and procedures that establish and present a good-faith effort to California State reviewers and auditors charged with any oversight responsibilities. California describes this as "reasonable security," but does not define this term; we will present a definition of "adequate security" aligned with the current NIST 800-171 definition within the State government.

What is "adequate security?" **Adequate security** is defined by "compliance" with the 110 NIST 800-171 security controls. It will also be considered adequate upon an authorization to operate[5] issued to the business or company by the State of California. This will most likely occur from the State Attorney General's Office[6] or by its designated proxy. Furthermore, this does not mean all security controls are in effect, but where a deviation is needed, a Plan of Action and Milestones (POAM) is provided.

A business must implement reasonable security procedures and practices that are appropriate to the nature of the personal information that is to be protected. A POAM is required as part of an official NIST 800-171 submission package and will be discussed in a later chapter. It should identify why the company cannot currently address, and when it expects to resolve the control. See Appendix C for a more detailed discussion or see the supplementary guide: *Writing an Effective Plan of Action & Milestones (POAM) available on Amazon® for further details.*

Past precedence and direction from the California Attorney General's Office in its 2016 *Data Breach Report*, suggested that companies that, for example, leverage the CIS's Critical Security Controls would likely meet the security requirements of the CCPA. The guidance did not discount companies and businesses from following equivalent, industry-recognized information security frameworks such as NIST 800-171. NIST 800-171 is the most understandable and most comfortable to adopt, and for that reason, we will suggest this is the best choice.

Additionally, NIST 800-series, in general, tell a business "what" is required; however, they do not help in describing "how" to meet the 110 security control requirements. This book provides both technical and administrative solutions to address each of the controls. All are acceptable approaches within the NIST Risk Management (RM) directives and are intended to quickly provide business owners and their IT staffs the ability to implement them swiftly. This book will provide a substantive start-point. It is designed to walk through the security controls in enough detail to ensure authorization to operate and conduct business specific to the CCPA.

More CCPA Specifics

The CCPA creates a private right of action for California residents if their personal information is subject to specific security incidents because of a business's failure to implement

---

[5] If the business fails to meet this standard within the proscribed timeframe, it is subject to not only civil penalties and fines, but likely suspension of its ability to operate within the State of California until such time it reaches compliance.

[6] Such means or mechanisms of how that will be accomplished have yet to be described.

reasonable security. Individuals may seek damages of $100 to $750 per consumer per incident. The CCPA also empowers the Attorney General to pursue cases against businesses for damages of up to $7,500 per **intentional**[7] violation on the part of the business.

The Attorney General has the authority to pursue civil actions against a company in violation of the CCPA. Businesses have 30 days to address a violation or be in breach of the CCPA and subject to fines; penalties range from $2,500 to $7,500 for each violation. The CCPA has yet to define what a violation entails; however, it can be assumed it will align with the federal interpretation of a good-faith effort on the part of the business. In other words, if the business can reasonably demonstrate it attempted to either address a control immediately or via a POAM, it would not be subject to penalty. (See the discussion above regarding "adequate security.")

Who is affected?

The CCPA restricts individual businesses and defines a "consumer" as any natural person who is a resident of California as defined in existing California tax provisions. Specifically, a "consumer" includes:

(1) An individual who is in California for other than a temporary or transitory purpose
(2) An individual who is domiciled in California to include from time to time is outside the State of California jurisdiction for a temporary or transitory purpose

What information is covered?

The CCPA expands the definition of "personal information" to include information that identifies, relates to, describes, is capable of being associated with, or could reasonably be linked with a consumer or household. This would include information, for example, an individual's name, physical address, social security number, education information, etc. The definition includes biometric data (e.g., iris scans, facial geometry, fingerprint data, etc.) collected without a consumer's knowledge.

Businesses may find that they collect information that may be considered sensitive under the CCPA even though other regulations or statutes may not classify it as such. The current belief is that the Attorney General (AG) will adopt regulations to revise various subcomponents of the definition of personal information dependent on any follow-on regulations or guidelines. The AG could further expand the definition beyond its already broad

---

[7] This book also provides specific direction to ensure a "good-faith" effort can be demonstrated and will likely be sufficient to avoid any punitive damages.

terms. Because of the breadth of these definitions, California businesses did not consider themselves subject to any requirement for maintaining regulated personal information.
Specific categories of information are **excluded** and include:

- o Publicly available information that is lawfully available from government records

- o Aggregated information that relates to a group or category of consumers. The individual's identity is removed or obfuscated in such a manner as to prevent traceability to a specified consumer

- o De-identified information that cannot reasonably relates to describing, etc., a consumer provided the businesses takes certain safeguards (*e.g.,* properly executing procedures to protect against reidentification by unauthorized third parties)

The Current Expansion and Impact of NIST 800-171

In 2019, the expectation is that the United States (US) federal government will expand the requirement further for NIST 800-171, and it will apply to the entirety of the federal government. It is already impacting many of the states as well to include New York, Massachusetts, and now California. It will require that any company, business, or agency, supporting the federal and state governments are compliant with NIST 800-171.

This book is specially designed for this pending challenge. It describes to the business owner "how" to implement the NIST 800-171 controls. It is not just about the technical solutions, but the regulatory approaches that are wholly acceptable under the principles of the Risk Management Framework (RMF). It is the precursor to potential and more compulsory obligations the private sector needs to abide by to protect the sensitivity and privacy of the citizenry's personal information. It is the first-step of much more to come as the challenges of hackers, and general threats to the US and the private sector become more pervasive. This book is focused not just on challenges, but how to effectively meet them in the coming years.

The Top 6 Immutable Elements of Effective RMF

NIST 800-171 is based on RMF, which is the standard across the federal government and is required by any company or organization wanting to sell products or services to the federal government. However, to be successful, there are six elements critical to full NIST 800-171 implementation. These are provided to better guide the reader and emphasize that RMF is leadership-driven—leadership must be as invested, if not more, than the IT division. These are based upon the authors over 20 years in security and is designed for the leader to engage with NIST 800-171 quickly and effectively.

1. **The Risk Management Framework (RMF) is risk-based, not threat-based.**

   What differentiates the National Institute of Standards and Technology (NIST)-created RMF from former cybersecurity frameworks is that it is about identifying, mitigating, and monitoring risk throughout the life of the Information Technology (IT) system. There are still strong arguments to return to a threat-focused model; however, it is unlikely to happen. Furthermore, an understanding of the capabilities of threat motives and capabilities are still an inherent sub-component of RMF in the form of the Risk Assessment Report (RAR), other internal, and external reporting awareness critical to effective cybersecurity.

   RMF is about time, money, and resources, and not necessarily about complete system security. The threat base—cyber-threats of many types and flavors-- has grown so large, that the only way to stay engaged with the current reactionary responses is through a balance of a company or agency limited resources in a risk-based approach.

2. **The Authorizing Official (AO)[8] accepts all residual risk – both responsible and accountable**

   The AO is the boss over not just the system, but the network that resides internal to the respective organization's firewall boundaries. The AO is regularly briefed (and should demand it) on the state of all security controls. The AO's interest must lie with whether they are 1) active—ultimately met under RMF controls, 2) mitigated—the controls are being met, but by other indirect measures such as policies, training measures, etc., or 3) not met—the control cannot be met technically (or in some cases financially) by the

---

[8] The AO is typically a senior executive or system "champion" that is aware of the strategic need and maintenance of the automated solution within the organization.

organization. There is NO partial credit in assessments, and the AO should at least quarterly be apprised of the state of cybersecurity for all systems residing within the AO's designated network boundary.

3. **The AO and System Owner (SO)[9] have a distinct supervisory connection to the system and each other**

The relationship between the AO and SO should be that of first-line supervision; however, that may not always be possible. At most, it should not exceed second-line supervision in order to provide direct leadership control and responsibility of the system under RMF. The problem with many organizations is that there is no direct connection between these two critical RMF positions. The AO needs to be able to influence the SO's regular evaluation process to ensure a focus on cybersecurity is complete and consistent.

4. **The SO is responsible for the daily security measures of the system**

The SO is the daily defender of the system. The SO's role is to continually ensure all security measures are met, and the IT environment is monitored for changes. While the AO is looking across the environment strategically, the SO is the tactical "commander" who makes sure all security measures are in place and working.

5. **It is not once and done...it's continuous monitoring**

At the core of RMF is Continuous Monitoring (ConMon). ConMon is the real foundation of the RMF. If you are not consistently monitoring the environment, you are not secure. For example, with the myriad of audit logs captured, they are seldom reviewed, and threats sparsely identified. Solutions like Smart Firewalls and Security Information Event Managers (SIEM) are first-generation solutions—but they are not enough. ConMon requires the active participation of cybersecurity professionals at all levels of the defense against potential cyber-attacks.

6. **It is all about the leadership—Really!**

Lastly, cybersecurity failures are not failures of the Chief Information Officer (CIO) or Chief Information Security Officer (CISO), but they are often the "sacrificial lambs" fired for a significant security breach. This mentality continues to contribute to cybersecurity failings where the community is leaving because of the lack of support and commitment from higher up to include the Chief Executive Officer (CEO) or Secretary of a federal

---

[9] The SO is usually a mid-level manager who understand the systems use and requirements. The SO is the tactical cybersecurity leader with direct control over resourcing and oversight of the deployed IT system.

agency. The responsibility and accountability must be centered at the highest senior of an organization, or cybersecurity breaches will continue without "pinning" accountability where it belongs.

The 2020 CCPA Cybersecurity Checklist

This checklist is provided to help offer significant security and privacy considerations for the business to begin planning for CCPA compliance. It should be used to orient the business' preliminary efforts for the employment of NIST 800-171 as a solution to meet the cybersecurity requirements of this NIST framework.

☐ **Does your business, company, or agency collect, maintain, or store California residents' personal information or if you have direct control over a subsidiary, sub-contractor, or third-party organization?**
- Direct or indirect control of the data is the first criterion to determine your responsibilities under the CCPA.

☐ **Do you have a Chief Information Officer, Privacy Officer, Chief Data Officer, etc., designated, in-writing, responsible for managing and protecting personal information?**
- *You need to designate one who has the background and ability to guide the business through the overall CCPA process and its requirements under NIST 800-171.*

☐ **Have you analyzed how personal information is ingested, processed, and shared within the company? Do you have a data flow diagram that shows information movement within the company's networks?**

☐ **How do you use NIST 800-171 to initially and through "continuous monitoring" activities ensure the proper security measures exist?**
- *What is security best-practices implemented to enhance and further secure sensitive personal information beyond NIST 800-171?*

☐ **How do you safeguard information in "transit" and "at-rest"? What encryption is in use? How is information redacted or obfuscated to enhance security and privacy?**

▪ Take actions to encrypt or redact consumers' personal information when collected, stored, and transmitted as a means of helping to mitigate some of the potential litigation burdens that could arise if unencrypted or unredacted personal information is the affected by a security incident.
▪ (See more of a discussion on Data in Transit (DIT) and Data at Rest (DAR) implementation in the **Access Control (AC)** chapter.

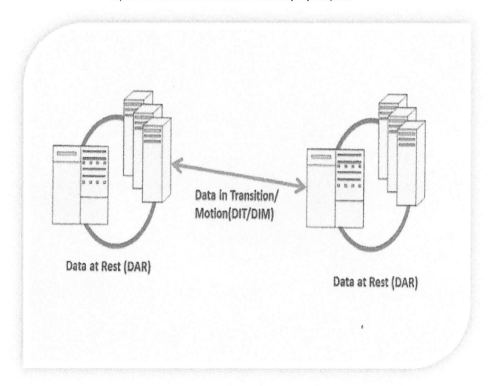

Data at Rest (DAR) versus Data in Transit/Motion (DIT/DIM) Conceptual Diagram

☐ **Did you plan for data segregation of California residents before implementation?**

        ▪ This will help when demonstrating to State official's compliance with the CCPA.

A Company's Cybersecurity Posture

The basis of NIST 800-171 is that businesses provide adequate security on all covered business Information Systems (IS). Typically, the minimum requirement to demonstrate control implementation is through **documentation**. Another term that is used throughout this book is an **artifact**. An artifact is any representation to a State official or independent third-party assessor that shows compliance with specific security controls. It is a significant part of the proof that a business owner would provide to the California government.

Artifacts are designed to support assertions of completeness, and we would suggest, for example, may include "screen-captures" as one of many proofs that a control is met; all modern Operating Systems (OS) include a "print screen" function where the text or image is captured, placed in temporary computer memory and can be inserted into a document application. This can then easily be provided to a "security control assessor" in the form of either a soft or hard copy artifact. IT personnel should use this function to show, for example, policy settings or system logging (audit) data. When in doubt, always have some form of graphical representation to show the government.

The common term for the collection of all applications and supporting artifacts is the Body of Evidence (BOE). The critical items required for the BOE includes three major items:

1. **Company Policy or Procedure.** For this book, these terms are used interchangeably. Virtually any direction provided to internal employees and subcontractors that are enforceable under US labor laws and Human Resource (HR) direction. It is recommended that such a policy or procedure artifact be a unique collection of how the company addresses each of the 110 security controls.

All cybersecurity-related policy or procedure requirements are best captured in a single policy or procedure guide. This should address the controls aligned with the security control families.

---

2. **System Security Plan (SSP).** This is a standard cybersecurity document. It describes the company's overall IT infrastructure to include hardware and software lists. Where appropriate, suggestions of additional artifacts that should be included in this document and duplicated into a standard SSP format will be recommended. (See *System Security Plan (SSP) Template and Workbook* "on Amazon®)

   A *free* 36-minute introduction to the SSP is currently available on Udemy.com at https://www.udemy.com/system-security-plan-ssp-for-nist-800-171-compliance/.

   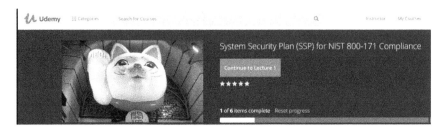

3. **Plans of Action and Milestones (POAM).** This describes any control that the company cannot fix or demonstrate its full compliance. It provides an opportunity for a company to delay addressing a difficult to implement a technical solution or because the cost may be prohibitive.

   The POAM will be used where the business cannot meet or address the control either for technical reasons, "we do not have a Data at Rest (DAR) encryption application," or cost, "we plan to purchase the DAR solution No Later Than April 1, 2022." POAMs should include milestones; milestones should describe what will be accomplished overtime to prepare for the full implementation of the control. What will the business do in the interim to address the control? This could include, for example, other mitigation responses of using improved physical security controls, such as a 24-7 guard force, the addition of a steel-door to prevent entry to the main computer servers or improved and enforceable policies that have explicit repercussions upon personnel.

   POAMs will always have a defined end date. Typically, it is either within 90 days, six months, or a year in length. One year should be the maximum date; however, the business, as part of this process, can request an extension to the POAM based on the "planned" end date; RMF affords flexibilities. Do not be afraid to exercise and use POAMs as appropriate. (See Access Control (AC) for a sample template).

POAMs typically should not be for more than a year; however, a critical hint, a company can request an <u>extension</u> multiple times if unable to fully meet the control.

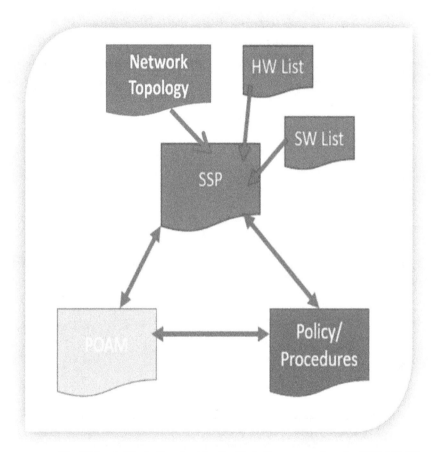

The Major Artifacts Required by the State Government under NIST 800-171

When working with the State Government, being simple moreover, consistent always help through a very young and less-than-defined process.

Minimum or More Complete?

A Cybersecurity mind-set

The focus is to provide the mental approach and technical understanding of what the control is (and what it is not). The first paragraph describes a MINIMUM ANSWER. This is what is needed to prepare a basic answer for a minimal and acceptable level of response. Mainly, these solutions require policy or procedural documents that describe to the State how the business will ensure this control will be met; if just trying to get through the process expeditiously, this paragraph will be enough to secure an approval.

If there is a greater desire to understand the process further and demonstrate a more substantial solution, the paragraph, MORE COMPLETE ANSWER is designed to provide more depth. It is intended to more completely describe to the business owner how to better show an understanding of its implementation of NIST 800-171.

Also, for clarification, the ***Basic Security Requirement*** heading is what is typically described as the **Common Control** for the control family. It is best to understand it is the significant control for the respective control family. The ***Derived Security Requirements*** can be considered more as supplemental and "more granular" requirements for the "parent" control. Depending on the types and kinds of data stored, these controls in the more *classic* NIST 800-53 publication can include hundreds of other controls.

FAMILY	FAMILY
(AC) Access Control	(MP) Media Protection
(AT) Awareness and Training	(PS) Personnel Security
(AU) Audit and Accountability	(PP) Physical Protection
(CM) Configuration Management	(RA) Risk Assessment
(IA) Identification and Authentication	(SA) Security Assessment
(IR) Incident Response	(SC) System and Communications Protection
(MA) Maintenance	(SI) System and Information Integrity

NIST 800-171 SECURITY REQUIREMENT FAMILIES

Tailoring-out Controls Possibilities

The 2016 version update to NIST 800-171, revision 1, provides a less-than-adequate direction on the matter of **control tailoring**. Tailoring is allowed and recommended where appropriate. Within the NIST 800-171, the concept of **tailoring-out** of control is desirable where technically or operationally it cannot be reasonably applied. This will require technical certainty that the control is Non-Applicable (N/A). Under this opportunity, if the company's IT architecture does not contain within its **security boundary,** the technology where such a control would be required to be applied then the control is identified as N/A.

For example, where the business has no Wi-Fi network in its security boundary, it can advise the State that any controls addressing the security of Wi-Fi networks would be an N/A control. The business cannot nor have reason to implement these security controls because it currently does not allow Wi-Fi networks or any presence of such equipment such as Wi-Fi routers, antennas, etc. The control would be marked as **compliant** and annotated as N/A at the time of the self-assessment. It would still be required to identify that Wi-fi is not currently authorized in the company's cybersecurity procedure guide or policy to properly document its absence as a suggested best-practice approach for the submitted BOE.

The following Wi-fi security controls most likely can be tailored-out specific to the company's existing IT infrastructure if there are no Wi-fi networks or devices.

1.1.16 Authorize wireless access before allowing such connections.

1.1.17 Protect wireless access using authentication and encryption.

Tailoring-out can be your friend

How to use this book?

In June 2018, the NIST issued NIST 800-171A, **"A**ssessing Security Requirements for Controlled Unclassified Information.**"** It increased the challenges and complexity of the current California State requirement to better secure the cybersecurity environment. It added another 298 sub-controls (SUB CTRL), also described within the cybersecurity community as a Control Correlation Identifier (CCI). The *CCI* provides a standard identifier and description for each of the singular and actionable statements that comprise a cybersecurity control or cybersecurity best practice. CCI bridges the gap between high-level policy expressions and low-level technical implementations. CCI allows a security requirement that is expressed in a high-level policy framework to be decomposed and explicitly associated with the low-level security setting(s) that must be assessed to determine compliance with the objectives of that specific security control.

The ability to trace security requirements from their origin (e.g., regulations, cybersecurity frameworks, etc.) to their low-level implementation allows organizations to readily demonstrate multiple cybersecurity compliance frameworks. CCI also provides a means to objectively rollup and compare related compliance assessment results across disparate technologies.

We have modified the original NIST 800-171A sub-control charts and have added a column to explain suggested approaches to answer the sub-control for a minimal 'compliant' status. We will not attempt to do more than that for this edition.

The generalized assessment from NIST 800-171A only describes an expanded framework and a starting point for developing more specific procedures to assess the security requirements in NIST 800-171 revision 1. *It does not add new controls; it only provides more detailed enhancements to the base control. There are still 110 controls.* (For the CCPA, these extended controls are not expected to be mandated by the AG, but a review of them is highly suggested as to be prepared if audited by the State or a designated assessment team).

Organizations have the flexibility to specialize in their assessment procedures by selecting the specific assessment methods and the set of assessment artifacts to achieve the assessment objectives. There is no expectation that all assessment methods and all artifacts will be used for every assessment. The assessment procedures and methods can be applied using multiple approaches to include self-assessment or independent, third-party assessments. Assessments may also be performed by sponsoring organizations (e.g., government agencies); such approaches may be specified in contracts or agreements by participating parties. Every effort has been attempted in this edition to provide additional information for the sub-control as needed.

Furthermore, assessments can be conducted by systems' developers, integrators, assessors, system owners, or their respective security staffs. Assessment teams combine available system information. System assessments can be used to compile and evaluate the evidence needed by organizations and to help determine the effectiveness of the safeguards implemented to protect personal information.

The following key is provided to add brevity where appropriate, and where the previous descriptions in Edition 1 remain complete for the purposes of answering the sub-control.

ACRONYM	MEANING	DESCRIPTION
NCR	No Change Required	The description and information in the base control are still correct, and there is no further need to modify the original administrative (policy) or technical recommendations.
P	Policy or Procedure	Requires an addition to the company's policy document to answer the sub-control; descriptions or examples are suggested as the "recommended approach" column.
T	A technical solution is needed	Identifies a technical solution is further needed to answer the control or mitigate (reduces) the vulnerability, but not necessarily completely.
PO	Plan of Action & Milestones	The suggestion here is for business owners, where the control appears to be technically challenging to implement, a POAM should be formulated; if able to address, it is always the *preferred* approach to answering any security control.
W	Waiver or Risk Acceptance	There are some situations—very long-term—where a waiver or risk acceptance, by the company, is a mechanism to accept risk for a control challenging to implement for several years due to lack of expertise, technologically or budget to fulfill the requirement

FINAL NOTE: The term Controlled Unclassified Information (CUI) found in NIST 800-171 may be considered equivalent to the term "personal or privacy information."

The NIST Control Families

ACCESS CONTROL (AC)
The most technical, complex, and vital

Access Control (AC) is probably the most technical and most vital security control family within the cybersecurity process. It is designed to focus computer support personnel, System Administrators (SA), or similar IT staff, on the technical security protections of critical data. This will include any CUI[10] and internal sensitive data maintained by the company's IT infrastructure and maintained by the company as part of doing business with the government. If making investments in cybersecurity infrastructure upgrades, the *AC control will provide the highest Return on Investment*.

Also, it is crucial to confirm whether either a technical solution is not already embedded in the current IT system. Many times, controls are ignored, captured by policy, or a POAM is developed, even though some base capabilities to address the control are already resident in the base system or more particularly within the network Operating System (OS). Also, check for accessory applications provided by the OS manufacturer to determine whether a no-cost solution is already resident. Ask the IT staff to confirm whether there is an existing technical solution as part of the system to avoid spending additional dollars for capabilities already in place.

Where cost is currently prohibitive to implement, a POAM is an acceptable but temporary solution. If unable to address the control during the company's "self-assessment" effort, then be prepared to formulate a Plans of Action and Milestone (POAM). (***Writing an Effective POAM*** is a current supplement to this book and is currently available on Amazon®).

---

[10] The term Controlled Unclassified Information (CUI) found in NIST 800-171 may be considered equivalent for the term "personal information."

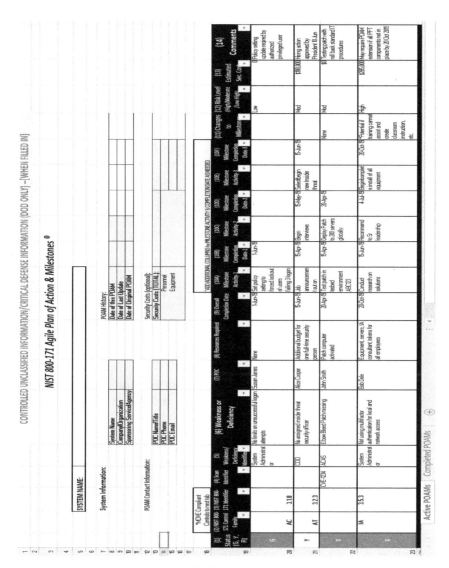

CONTROLLED UNCLASSIFIED INFORMATION/CRITICAL DEFENSE INFORMATION [DOD ONLY] – [WHEN FILLED IN]

NIST 800-171 Agile Plan of Action & Milestones ®

SYSTEM NAME:

System Information:
System Name
Company/Organization
Sponsoring Service/Agency

POAM Contact Information:
POC Name/Title
POC Phone
POC Email

POAM History:
Date of this POAM
Date of Last Update
Date of Original POAM

Security Costs (optional):
Security Costs [TOTAL]:
Personnel
Equipment

POAM Template

(Template available at https://cybersentinel.tech in the "Cybershop" for purchase)

Basic Security Requirements:

3.1.1 Limit information system access to authorized users, processes acting on behalf of authorized users, or devices (including other information systems).
MINIMUM ANSWER: Address this control in the business policy/procedural document. (See example procedure below).

It should identify the types of users and what level of access they are authorized. Typically, there are **general users** who have regular daily access to the corporate system data and **elevated/privileged users**.

Elevated/privileged users are usually limited to, for example, System Administrators (SA), Database Administrators (DBA), and other designated Help Desk IT support staff personnel who manage the back-office care of the system; these users usually have **root access**. Root access provides what is more typically described as **super-user** access. These individuals should be highly and regularly screened. These individuals need to be regularly assessed or audited by senior corporate designated personnel.

MORE COMPLETE ANSWER: This should include screen captures that show a sample of employees and their types and kinds of access rights. This could include their read, write, edit, delete, etc., **rights** typically controlled by an assigned SA.

We have provided an example of a suggested procedure for this control:

> EXAMPLE PROCEDURE: *The company has defined two types of authorized users. There are **general users**, those that require regular daily access to company automated resources, and **privileged users**, employees with elevated privileges required to conduct regular back-office care and maintenance of corporate assets and Information Technology (IT) systems. Access to the company's [example] financial, ordering, and human resource systems will be restricted to those general users with a need, based upon their duties, to access these systems. Immediate supervisors will validate their need and advise the IT Help Desk to issue appropriate access credentials [login identification and password] after completing "Cybersecurity Awareness Training." User credentials will not be shared and...."*

ASSESSMENT OBJECTIVE *Determine if:*		
SUB-CTRL	*DESCRIPTION*	**RECOMMENDED APPROACH**
3.1.1[a]	*Authorized users are identified.*	NCR
3.1.1[b]	*Processes acting on behalf of authorized users are identified.*	*P-Processes need to by further defined. This should include access to major applications and their functionality, e.g., finance for finance personnel only, contracting for contract personnel; also, some supervisors will require access to these functional "processes" for oversight purposes.*
3.1.1[c]	*Devices (and other systems) authorized to connect to the system are identified.*	SSP-Should identifies all devices internal to the security boundary as the primary source document.
3.1.1[d]	*System access is limited to authorized users.*	NCR
3.1.1[e]	*System access is limited to processes acting on behalf of authorized users.*	P-Update policy document that states "system access is limited to processes acting on behalf of authorized users."
3.1.1[f]	*System access is limited to authorized devices (including other systems).*	P/SSP-State in policy document; should align with SSP.

ASSESSMENT METHOD AND OBJECTS

Examine: [*SELECT FROM:* Access control policy; procedures addressing account management; system security plan; system design documentation; system configuration settings and associated documentation; list of active system accounts and the name of the individual associated with each account; notifications or records of recently transferred, separated, or terminated employees; list of conditions for group and role membership; list of recently disabled system accounts along with the name of the individual associated with each account; access authorization records; account management compliance reviews; system monitoring records; system audit logs and records; list of devices and systems authorized to connect to organizational systems; other relevant documents or records].

3.1.2 Limit information system access to the types of transactions and functions that authorized users are permitted to execute.

MINIMUM ANSWER: Address this control in the business policy/procedural document. It should identify the types of transactions and what level is allowed for authorized users. Elevated or privileged users have access to back-office maintenance and care of the network such as account creation, database maintenance, etc.; privileged users can also have universal access, but different logins and passwords should segregate their privileges for audit purposes.

MORE COMPLETE ANSWER: This could include a screen capture that shows a sample of employees and their types and kinds of rights. This would include their read, write, edit, delete, etc., rights typically controlled by assigned SA. The SA should be able to provide the hardcopy printouts for inclusion into the final submission packet to the contract office or their designated recipient.

ASSESSMENT OBJECTIVE *Determine if:*		
SUB-CTRL	*DESCRIPTION*	**RECOMMENDED APPROACH**
3.1.2[a]	*The types of transactions and functions that authorized users are permitted to execute are defined.*	NCR
3.1.2[b]	*System access is limited to the defined types of transactions and functions for authorized users.*	NCR
ASSESSMENT METHODS AND CANDIDATE ARTIFACTS FOR REVIEW		
Examine: [*SELECT FROM:* Access control policy; procedures addressing access enforcement; system security plan; system design documentation; list of approved authorizations including remote access authorizations; system audit logs and records; system configuration settings and associated documentation; other relevant documents or records].		
Test: [*SELECT FROM:* Mechanisms implementing access control policy].		

Derived (Supplemental) Security Requirements:

3.1.3 Control the flow of CUI flowing the approved authorizations.
MINIMUM ANSWER: Companies typically use **flow control** policies and technologies to manage the movement of CUI throughout the IT architecture; flow control is based on the types of information.

In terms of procedural updates, discussion of the corporate documents should address several areas of concern: 1) That only authorized personnel within the company with the requisite need-to-know are provided access; 2) appropriate security measures are in place to include encryption while Data is in Transit (DIT); 3) what are the procedures for handling internal employees who violate these company rules?; and, 4) how does the company alert the federal government if there is external access (hackers) to its IT infrastructure and its CUI?

MORE COMPLETE ANSWER: Addressing this control can further be demonstrated by implementing training (See Awareness and Training (AT) control) as a form of **mitigation**; mitigation are other supporting efforts, not just technical, that can reduce the effects of a threat exploits this control. The company could also include risk from insider threats (See Control 3.2.3 for discussion of "insider threat.") by requiring employees to complete Non-disclosure (NDA) and non-compete agreements (NCA). These added measures *reduce or mitigate the risk to the IT infrastructure*. They should also address employees that depart, resign, or are terminated by the company; the consideration is for disgruntled employees that may depart the company with potentially sensitive CUICDI.

Flow control could also be better shown to a State government assessor in terms of a technical solution. This could be further demonstrated by using encryption for DIT and Data at Rest (DAR). These encryption requirements within NIST 800-171 necessitate differing technical solutions, and Federal Information Processing Standards (FIPS) 140-2 compliance; see Control 3.13.11 for more detail.

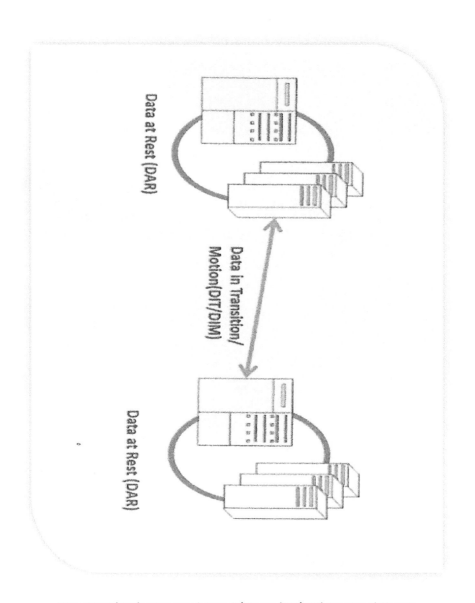

Data at Rest (DAR) versus Data in Transit/Motion (DIT/DIM) Conceptual Diagram

The answer could also include weekly reviews of access logs. Typically, IT support personnel or the SA would conduct recurring audits. If anomalies are detected, what is the procedure to alert senior management to personnel attempting access to CUI and other sensitive data? This offers a more significant demonstration of company security measures to government representatives.

SUB-CTRL	DESCRIPTION	RECOMMENDED APPROACH
ASSESSMENT OBJECTIVE: *Determine if:*		
3.1.3[a]	*Information flow control policies are defined.*	NCR
3.1.3[b]	*Methods and enforcement mechanisms for controlling the flow of CUI are defined.*	NCR (P-especially FIPS 140-2 encryption standards).
3.1.3[c]	*Designated sources and destinations (e.g., networks, individuals, and devices) for CUI within the system and between interconnected systems are identified.*	P/SSP-Add an update to policy/procedure document and a "data flow" diagram to SSP that describes what the flow from the originator to destination involves. At each source or destination, identify whether the data is encrypted or not.
3.1.3[d]	*Authorizations for controlling the flow of CUI are defined.*	NCR
3.1.3[e]	*Approved authorizations for controlling the flow of CUI are enforced.*	P-Updates to the policy should identify the individual or body that can make approved changes to "data flow."

ASSESSMENT METHODS AND CANDIDATE ARTIFACTS FOR REVIEW

Examine: [*SELECT FROM:* Access control policy; information flow control policies; procedures addressing information flow enforcement; system security plan; system design documentation; system configuration settings and associated documentation; list of information flow authorizations; system baseline configuration; system audit logs and records; other relevant documents or records].

Test: [*SELECT FROM:* Mechanisms implementing information flow enforcement policy].

3.1.4 Separate the duties of individuals to reduce the risk of malicious activity without collusion.

MINIMUM ANSWER: This should be described in the corporate cybersecurity procedural document and should identify the roles and responsibilities of how oversight will be executed. When this is difficult, based on the size and limited IT personnel, a POAM is highly recommended.

The POAM should suggest other ways used to mitigate such a **risk**, and potentially look at both human and automated means to better address in the future.

MORE COMPLETE ANSWER: Individuals should be assigned *in-writing* and their roles and responsibilities. This could also include the reporting thresholds of unauthorized activities and who is alerted internal threats; this would better provide a more defined solution. It also could address Human Resource (HR) challenges when such incidents occur and provide a means of action against violators of corporate policy.

ASSESSMENT OBJECTIVE *Determine if:*		
SUB-CTRL	*DESCRIPTION*	**RECOMMENDED APPROACH**
3.1.4[a]	*The duties of individuals requiring separation are defined.*	NCR
3.1.4[b]	*Responsibilities for duties that require separation are assigned to separate individuals.*	NCR
3.1.4[c]	*Access privileges that enable individuals to exercise the duties that require separation are granted to separate individuals.*	NCR

3.1.5 Employ the principle of least privilege, including for specific security functions and privileged accounts.

MINIMUM ANSWER: The principle of least privilege is a vital cybersecurity tenet. The concept of least privilege is about allowing only authorized access for users and processes that they have direct responsibility. It is limited to only a necessary level of access to accomplish tasks for specific business functions. This should be described in the corporate cybersecurity policy document. This should also be part of necessary user agreements to include what is described in government terminology an **Acceptable Use Policy** (AUP).

MORE COMPLETE ANSWER: Much like the controls described above, a sampling of employees' print-outs or screen captures could show selected and authorized individual rights. A sampling, especially of privileged users, and their assigned roles within the company's IT infrastructure would be a target of potential third-party government assessors. This would be used by assessors to support the developing NIST 800-171 certification process.

ASSESSMENT OBJECTIVE *Determine if:*		
SUB-CTRL	*DESCRIPTION*	RECOMMENDED APPROACH
3.1.5[a]	*Privileged accounts are identified.*	P-Should has a list of privileged users as an ongoing artifact.
3.1.5[b]	*Access to privileged accounts is authorized in accordance with the principle of least privilege.*	NCR
3.1.5[c]	*Security functions are identified.*	NCR
3.1.5[d]	*Access to security functions is authorized in accordance with the principle of least privilege.*	NCR

3.1.6 Use non-privileged accounts or roles when accessing nonsecurity functions.

MINIMUM ANSWER: It is best to always first answer controls from a policy or procedural solution. Substantially, this is preventing "general users" from accessing the corporate infrastructure and creating accounts, deleting databases, or elevating their privileges to gain access to both CUI and sensitive corporate data. This is about providing the least amount of access and privilege based upon the duties assigned. Companies will see the control below that mandates a separation not just of duties, but access as well based on position and a clear need-to-know.

MORE COMPLETE ANSWER: The more-complete answer could be through automated solutions that monitor access to other security functions such as password resets, account creation, etc. This could include logging and review of all system access. It could also include automated tools that restrict access based upon a user's rights. These technical settings within the tool are established by company policy and monitored by, for example, the local SA.

ASSESSMENT OBJECTIVE *Determine if:*		
SUB-CTRL	*DESCRIPTION*	**RECOMMENDED APPROACH**
3.1.6[a]	*Nonsecurity functions are identified.*	NCR
3.1.6[b]	*Users are required to use non-privileged accounts or roles when accessing nonsecurity functions.*	P-This statement should be part of the company policy: *"Users are required to use non-privileged accounts or roles when accessing nonsecurity functions." (Best way to ensure completeness).*

3.1.7 Prevent non-privileged users from executing privileged functions and audit the execution of such functions.

MINIMUM ANSWER: There are many apparent similarities of the controls, and that was initially designed into NIST 800-171 for a reason. Security controls are supposed to be reinforcing, and this control is only slightly different in its scope than others described earlier.

Control 3.1.6 is similar is reinforcing this control as well as others. The company's procedure guide can explicitly "rewrite" the original control description: "Prevent non-privileged users from executing privileged functions...." An example procedure write-up based upon the original control description is provided:

> EXAMPLE PROCEDURE: *Non-privileged users are prohibited from executing any privileged functions or system audits without the authority of the company's Chief Operating Officer, Chief Information Security Officer, or their designated representative. All requests will be submitted in writing with their first-line supervisor validating the need for such access for a limited and specified time.*

Additionally, this procedure limits higher-order (privileged) functions such as creating accounts for others, deleting database files, etc. It also requires the auditing of all privileged functions. It is suggested that the assigned SA at least weekly review and report inconsistencies of non-privileged/general users attempting (and, hopefully failing) to access parts of the internal infrastructure.

MORE COMPLETE ANSWER: A more thorough representation would be to provide copies of audit logs that include who, when, and what were the results of an audit evaluation; these artifacts should demonstrate that the company is following its internal cybersecurity procedures.

NOTE ABOUT "FREQUENCY": Many of the controls do not define how often a business should conduct a review, reassessment, etc. The business owner can "define success," for example, to the State government Contract Office or cybersecurity assessor. The critical consideration is that the business determines the frequency of reviews, in general, based upon the perceived or actual sensitivity of the data. This book will typically provide the more stringent government frequency standard, but nothing prevents a company from conducting less often reviews if it can be substantiated.

ASSESSMENT OBJECTIVE *Determine if:*		
SUB-CTRL	*DESCRIPTION*	**RECOMMENDED APPROACH**
3.1.7[a]	*Privileged functions are defined.*	NCR
3.1.7[b]	*Non-privileged users are defined.*	NCR
3.1.7[c]	*Non-privileged users are prevented from executing privileged functions.*	NCR
3.1.7[d]	*The execution of privileged functions is captured in audit logs.*	P- Example policy statement update might read as: *"privileged functions are always captured and reviewed within audit logs weekly."*

POTENTIAL ASSESSMENT METHODS AND CANDIDATE ARTIFACTS FOR REVIEW

Examine: [*SELECT FROM:* Access control policy; procedures addressing least privilege; system security plan; system design documentation; list of privileged functions and associated user account assignments; system configuration settings and associated documentation; system audit logs and records; other relevant documents or records].

Test: [*SELECT FROM:* Mechanisms implementing least privilege functions for non-privileged users; mechanisms auditing the execution of privileged functions].

"Define your own success."

3.1.8 Limit unsuccessful logon attempts.

MINIMUM ANSWER: Government standard policy is after three failed logins the system will automatically lock out the individual. Suggest this should be no more than five failed logins, especially if employees are not computer savvy. This requires both the technical solution by the corporate IT system and described in the corporate procedure guide.

MORE COMPLETE ANSWER: For example, the additional ability to provide a screen capture that provides an artifact showing what happens when an employee reaches the maximum number of logins would meet this control; this could be added to the submission packet. It is also vital to document procedures to include the process to regain network access.

ASSESSMENT OBJECTIVE *Determine if:*		
SUB-CTRL	*DESCRIPTION*	**RECOMMENDED APPROACH**
3.1.8[a]	*The means of limiting unsuccessful logon attempts is defined.*	T-This is looking for what is monitoring unsuccessful logons. It could be as necessary as: "The XYZ Operating System enforces failed logon attempts after three fails."
3.1.8[b]	*The defined means of limiting unsuccessful logon attempts is implemented.*	T-(See above)

POTENTIAL ASSESSMENT METHODS AND CANDIDATE ARTIFACTS FOR REVIEW
Examine: [*SELECT FROM:* Access control policy; procedures addressing unsuccessful logon attempts; system security plan; system design documentation; system configuration settings and associated documentation; system audit logs and records; other relevant documents or records].
Test: [*SELECT FROM:* Mechanisms implementing access control policy for unsuccessful logon attempts].

3.1.9 Provide privacy and security notices consistent with applicable CUI rules.

MINIMUM ANSWER: Provided below is a current version of a **Warning Banner** designed for company purposes. It should either be physically posted on or near each terminal or on the on-screen logon (preferred); this should also always include consent to monitoring. Recommend consulting with a legal representative for final approval and dissemination to employees.

[Company] Warning Banner

Use of this or any other [Company name] computer system constitutes consent to monitoring at all times.

This is a [Company name] computer system. All [Company name] computer systems and related equipment are intended for the communication, transmission, processing, and storage of official or other authorized information only. All [Company name] computer systems are subject to monitoring at all times to ensure the proper functioning of equipment and systems including security devices and systems, to prevent unauthorized use and violations of statutes and security regulations, to deter criminal activity, and for other similar purposes. Any user of a [Company name] computer system should be aware that any information placed in the system is subject to monitoring and is not subject to any expectation of privacy.

If monitoring of this or any other [Company name] computer system reveals possible evidence of the violation of criminal statutes, this evidence, and any other related information, including identification information about the user, may be provided to law enforcement officials. If monitoring of this or any other [Company name] computer systems reveals violations of security regulations or unauthorized use, employees who violate security regulations or make unauthorized use of [Company name] computer systems are subject to appropriate disciplinary action.

Use of this or any other [Company name] computer system constitutes consent to monitoring at all times.

MORE COMPLETE ANSWER: Another consideration should be that this policy also is coordinated with Human Resources (HR). This could further include that all employees sign a copy of this notice, and it is placed in their official file. Select and redacted copies could be used to demonstrate an active adherence to this requirement as a sampling provided to the government. It could also potentially describe how the company can take actions against personnel who fail or violate this warning.

ASSESSMENT OBJECTIVE *Determine if:*		
SUB-CTRL	*DESCRIPTION*	**RECOMMENDED APPROACH**
3.1.9[a]	*Privacy and security notices required by CUI-specified rules are identified, consistent, and associated with the specific CUI category.*	NCR
3.1.9[b]	*Privacy and security notices are displayed.*	NCR (This can be either physically displayed or when logging in [preferred]).

POTENTIAL ASSESSMENT METHODS AND CANDIDATE ARTIFACTS FOR REVIEW

Examine: [*SELECT FROM:* Privacy and security policies, procedures addressing system use notification; documented approval of system use notification messages or banners; system audit logs and records; system design documentation; user acknowledgements of notification message or banner; system security plan; system use notification messages; system configuration settings and associated documentation; other relevant documents or records].

Test: [*SELECT FROM:* Mechanisms implementing system use notification].

3.1.10. Use session lock with pattern-hiding displays to prevent access/viewing of data after a period of inactivity.

MINIMUM ANSWER: While this may appear as solely a technical solution, it too should be identified in the company policy or procedure document. Session lock describes the period of inactivity when a computer terminal will automatically lock out the user. Suggest no more than 10 minutes for a computer lockout. Selecting longer is acceptable based upon many factors such as the type of work done (e.g., finance personnel) or the physical security level of the business (e.g., a restricted area with a limited number of authorized employees) is acceptable. However, be prepared to defend the balance between the company's need to meet government mission requirements and the risks of excessive session lock timeouts.

Secondarily, **Pattern Hiding** is desired to prevent the concept of "shoulder surfing." Other like terms that are synonymous include **masking** and **obfuscation**.

Pattern hiding is designed to prevent an individual from observing an employee typing their password or Personal Identification Number (PIN). This control could include asterisks (*), for example, that mask the correct information. This prevents insiders or even visitors from "stealing" another user's login credentials.

Password without Pattern Hiding: PA$$w0rD

Password with Pattern Hiding: ********

Pattern Hiding

MORE COMPLETE ANSWER: The better solution could include much shorter periods for a time-out, and longer password length and complexity; the standard is at least 15 alpha-numeric and special characters.

- Alpha: abcde….
- Numeric: 12345…
- Special Characters: @ # $ % ….

(See Control 3.13.10 for a further discussion of **Multifactor Authentication (MFA)** and **Two Factor Authentication (2FA))**.

As an ongoing reminder, it is critical to place artifacts describing the technical solution demonstrated, for example, using screen capture. It should be transparent and easily traceable to this control's implementation by an audit representative or assessor.

ASSESSMENT OBJECTIVE *Determine if:*		
SUB-CTRL	*DESCRIPTION*	**RECOMMENDED APPROACH**
3.1.10[a]	*The period of inactivity after which the system initiates a session lock is defined.*	NCR
3.1.10[b]	*Access to the system and viewing of data is prevented by initiating a session lock after the defined period of inactivity.*	NCR
3.1.10[c]	*Previously visible information is concealed via a pattern-hiding display*	NCR

	after the defined period of inactivity.	

POTENTIAL ASSESSMENT METHODS AND CANDIDATE ARTIFACTS FOR REVIEW

Examine: [*SELECT FROM:* Access control policy; procedures addressing session lock; procedures addressing identification and authentication; system design documentation; system configuration settings and associated documentation; system security plan; other relevant documents or records].

Test: [*SELECT FROM:* Mechanisms implementing access control policy for session lock].

3.1.11. Terminate (automatically) a user session after a defined condition.

MINIMUM ANSWER: The simplest solution is a setting that the SA or other designated IT personnel, sets within the network's operating and management applications. Typically, most network operating systems can be set to enforce a terminal/complete lockout. This control implementation completely logs out the user and terminates any communications' sessions to include, for example, access to corporate databases, financial systems, or the Internet. It requires employees to re-initiate session connections to the network after this more-complete session logout occurs.

MORE COMPLETE ANSWER: The complete answer could include screen captures of policy settings for session terminations and time-outs. The SA or designated company representative should be able to provide as an artifact.

ASSESSMENT OBJECTIVE *Determine if:*		
SUB-CTRL	*DESCRIPTION*	**RECOMMENDED APPROACH**
3.1.11[a]	*Conditions requiring a user session to terminate are defined.*	NCR
3.1.11[b]	*A user session is automatically terminated after any of the defined conditions occur.*	NCR

POTENTIAL ASSESSMENT METHODS AND CANDIDATE ARTIFACTS FOR REVIEW

Examine: [*SELECT FROM:* Access control policy; procedures addressing session termination; system design documentation; system security plan; system configuration settings and associated documentation; list of conditions or trigger events requiring session disconnect; system audit logs and records; other relevant documents or records].

Test: [*SELECT FROM:* Mechanisms implementing user session termination].

3.1.12 Monitor and control remote access sessions.

MINIMUM ANSWER: This control is about remote access where one computer can control another computer over the Internet. This may include desktop support personnel "remoting into" an employee's computer to update the latest version of Firefox ® or a work-at-home employee inputting financial data into the corporate finance system. Identify these types of access as part of the procedural guide and describe who is authorized, how their access is limited (such as a finance employee cannot issue themselves a corporate check), and the repercussions of violating the policy.

MORE COMPLETE ANSWER: The better technological approach could include restrictions to only IT help personnel using remote capabilities. Company policy should require regular review of auditable events and logs. A screen capture would be helpful to show the policy settings specific to the remote desktop application.

ASSESSMENT OBJECTIVE *Determine if:*		
SUB-CTRL	*DESCRIPTION*	RECOMMENDED APPROACH
3.1.12[a]	*Remote access sessions are permitted.*	P-Only for authorized personnel with a clear need
3.1.12[b]	*The types of permitted remote access are identified.*	NCR
3.1.12[c]	*Remote access sessions are controlled.*	NCR
3.1.12[d]	*Remote access sessions are monitored.*	P-Recommend that these sessions be logged for all users.

POTENTIAL ASSESSMENT METHODS AND CANDIDATE ARTIFACTS FOR REVIEW

Examine: [*SELECT FROM:* Access control policy; procedures addressing remote access implementation and usage (including restrictions); configuration management plan; system security plan; system design documentation; system configuration settings and associated documentation; remote access authorizations; system audit logs and records; other relevant documents or records].

Test: [*SELECT FROM:* Remote access management capability for the system].

3.1.13 Employ cryptographic mechanisms to protect the confidentiality of remote access sessions.

MINIMUM ANSWER: *This is a Data in Transit (DIT) issue*. Ensure the procedure requires the company's solution only uses approved cryptographic solutions. The **Advanced Encryption Standard** (AES) is considered the current standard for encryption within the State government. Also, use the 256 kilobytes (kb) key length versions.

There are many commercial solutions in this area. Major software companies provide solutions that secure DIT and are typically at reasonable prices for small business options such as Symantec ®, McAfee ®, and Microsoft®.

Again, document, document, document

MORE COMPLETE ANSWER: (See Control 3.1.3 for a more detailed representation). It is usually a capability directly afforded by the remote access application tool providers. The more critical issue within the government is whether the application tool company ensures the application is coming from a US-based software developer.

There are many overseas developers, for example, to include Russia, former Warsaw Pact countries, and China, that are of concern to the US government. The apprehension is about commercial products from these nations and their potential threat to US national security. The business should confirm that the product is coming from a current ally of the US; these would include the United Kingdom, Australia, etc. *Before purchasing, ensure you have done your homework, and provide proof the remote access software is accepted by the State government.*

ASSESSMENT OBJECTIVE *Determine if:*		
SUB-CTRL	*DESCRIPTION*	**RECOMMENDED APPROACH**
3.1.13[a]	*Cryptographic mechanisms to*	NCR

		protect the confidentiality of remote access sessions are identified.	
3.1.13[b]		Cryptographic mechanisms to protect the confidentiality of remote access sessions are implemented.	NCR

ASSESSMENT METHODS AND CANDIDATE ARTIFACTS FOR REVIEW

Examine: [*SELECT FROM:* Access control policy; procedures are addressing remote access to the system; system security plan; system design documentation; system configuration settings and associated documentation; cryptographic mechanisms and associated configuration documentation; system audit logs and records; other relevant documents or records].

Test: [*SELECT FROM:* Cryptographic mechanisms protecting remote access sessions].

3.1.14 Route remote access via managed access control points.

MINIMUM ANSWER: **Managed access control** points are about control of traffic through "trusted" connections. For example, this could be Verizon ® or AT&T® as the company's Internet Service Provider (ISP). It would be highly recommended to include any contracted services or Service Level Agreements (SLA) from these providers. They may include additional threat and spam filtering services that could reduce the "bad guys" from gaining access to corporate data; these are ideal artifacts for proof of satisfactorily meeting this control.

MORE COMPLETE ANSWER: Another addition could also be using what is called a **Virtual Private Network (VPN).** These are also essential services the major providers have for additional costs.

Describing and providing such agreements could also identify a **defense in depth** approach; the first level is through the VPN service, and the second would be provided by the remote access software providing an additional layer of defense. Defense in depth can include such protective efforts to prevent unauthorized access to company IT assets:

- Physical protection (e.g., alarms, guards)
- Perimeter (e.g., firewalls, Intrusion Detection System (IDS), "Trusted Internet Connections")
- Application/Executables (e.g., **whitelisting** of authorized software, **blacklisting** blocking specified programs)

- Data (e.g., Data Loss Protection programs, Access controls, auditing)

ASSESSMENT OBJECTIVE *Determine if:*		
SUB-CTRL	***DESCRIPTION***	**RECOMMENDED APPROACH**
3.1.14[a]	*Managed access control points are identified and implemented.*	NCR
3.1.14[b]	*Remote access is routed through managed network access control points.*	NCR

POTENTIAL ASSESSMENT METHODS AND CANDIDATE ARTIFACTS FOR REVIEW

Examine: [*SELECT FROM:* Access control policy; procedures are addressing remote access to the system; system security plan; system design documentation; list of all managed network access control points; system configuration settings and associated documentation; system audit logs and records; other relevant documents or records].

Test: [*SELECT FROM:* Mechanisms routing all remote accesses through managed network access control points].

3.1.15 Authorize remote execution of privileged commands and remote access to security-relevant information.

MINIMUM ANSWER: NIST 800-53 is the base document for all controls of NIST 800-171. It describes what businesses should manage and authorize privileged access to **security-relevant** information (e.g., finance information, IP, etc.), and using remote access only for "compelling operational needs."

This would explicitly be documented in the restrictions of who and under what circumstances security-relevant information may be accessed by company personnel. The base NIST control requires the business to documents the rationale for this access in the System Security Plan (SSP); the interpretation is that the corporate cybersecurity policy should be an annex or appendix to the **SSP**. (See *System Security Plan (SSP) Template and Workbook"* on Amazon®)

MORE COMPLETE ANSWER: The ideal artifact suggested are the logs of remote access within and external to the company. This could also be found in the firewall audit logs as well as the remote access software application logs for comparison; these could also be used to identify log modifications that may be an indicator of **insider threat**. (See Control 3.2.3 for further discussion of this topic area).

ASSESSMENT OBJECTIVE *Determine if:*		
SUB-CTRL	*DESCRIPTION*	**RECOMMENDED APPROACH**
3.1.15[a]	*Privileged commands authorized for remote execution are identified.*	P-Updates to policy should identify those "commands" that could compromise data such as changing prices, for example, without a requisite second party review, i.e., "separation of duties."
3.1.15[b]	*Security-relevant information authorized to be accessed remotely is identified.*	NCR
3.1.15[c]	*The execution of the identified privileged commands via remote access is authorized.*	NCR
3.1.15[d]	*Access to the identified security-relevant information via remote access is authorized.*	NCR

ASSESSMENT METHODS AND CANDIDATE ARTIFACTS FOR REVIEW
Examine: [*SELECT FROM:* Access control policy; procedures addressing remote access to the system; system configuration settings and associated documentation; system security plan; system audit logs and records; other relevant documents or records].

Test: [*SELECT FROM:* Mechanisms implementing remote access management].

3.1.16 Authorize wireless access prior to allowing such connections.

MINIMUM ANSWER: This would include wireless access agreements and more commonly describe earlier is an Acceptable Use Policy (AUP). For example, an AUP would include defining the types and kinds of sites restricted from access by employees. These are typically gambling, pornography sites, etc. AUP's should be reviewed by a lawyer before requiring employees to sign.

MORE COMPLETE ANSWER: The more-complete technical solution could identify unapproved sites and prevent "guest" access. (While guest access is not recommended, it is better to establish a secondary Wi-Fi network to accommodate and restrict visitors and third-party personnel from having direct access to the company network.)

It is also essential that the Wi-Fi's network topology and encryption standard be provided as an artifact to the government once the final packet is ready for submission. This should be part of the SSP and the corporate cybersecurity procedure document.

ASSESSMENT OBJECTIVE *Determine if:*		
SUB-CTRL	*DESCRIPTION*	**RECOMMENDED APPROACH**
3.1.16[a]	*Wireless access points are identified.*	NCR (Specifically, part of the SSP)
3.1.16[b]	*Wireless access is authorized prior to allow such connections.*	NCR

POTENTIAL ASSESSMENT METHODS AND CANDIDATE ARTIFACTS FOR REVIEW
Examine: [*SELECT FROM:* Access control policy; configuration management plan; procedures addressing wireless access implementation and usage (including restrictions); system security plan; system design documentation; system configuration settings and associated documentation; wireless access authorizations; system audit logs and records; other relevant documents or records].
Test: [*SELECT FROM:* Wireless access management capability for the system].

3.1.17 Protect wireless access using authentication and encryption.

MINIMUM ANSWER: Ensure this is included in the corporate procedure or policy that only authorized personnel within the firm to have access and that the appropriate level of encryption is in place. Currently, the 802.11 standards are used, and Wi-Fi Protected Access 2 (WPA2) encryption should be the minimum standard.

MORE COMPLETE ANSWER: Use of Wi-Fi "sniffing technology" while available may be prohibitively costly to smaller businesses. This technology can identify and audit unauthorized entry into the wireless portion of the network and subsequently provides access to the "physical" company network. Sniffers can be used to notify security personnel either through email or Short Message Service (SMS)-text alerts of such intrusions; if company data is highly sensitive, then this investment may be necessary. Also, maintain any documentation about the "sniffer" and its capabilities; provide it to government representatives as part of the official submission.

ASSESSMENT OBJECTIVE *Determine if:*		
SUB-CTRL	*DESCRIPTION*	**RECOMMENDED APPROACH**
3.1.17[a]	*Wireless access to the system is protected using authentication.*	NCR
3.1.17[b]	*Wireless access to the system is protected using encryption.*	NCR

ASSESSMENT METHODS AND CANDIDATE ARTIFACTS FOR REVIEW

Examine: [*SELECT FROM:* Access control policy; system design documentation; procedures addressing wireless implementation and usage (including restrictions); system security plan; system configuration settings and associated documentation; system audit logs and records; other relevant documents or records].

Test: [*SELECT FROM:* Mechanisms implementing wireless access protections to the system].

3.1.18. Control connection of mobile devices.

MINIMUM ANSWER: Most businesses' mobile devices are their cell phones. This would also include laptops and computer "pads" with web-enabled capabilities. This would first require as a matter of policy that employees only use secure connections for their devices when not using the company's service provider—these should be verified as secure. This would also explicitly bar employees use of unsecured Wi-fi **hot spots** such as fast-food restaurants, coffee shops, etc. Home Wi-fi networks are typically secure but ensure that employees know to select **WPA2** as their standard at-home secure connection protocol.

MORE COMPLETE ANSWER: A better way to demonstrate this control is by discussing with the cell phone provider the ability to prevent corporate phones from using insecure Wi-Fi networks at any time. The provider should be able to block access if the mobile phone does not "see" or recognize a secure connection. Include any proof from service agreements of such a provision as part of the submitted BOE.

ASSESSMENT OBJECTIVE *Determine if:*		
SUB-CTRL	*DESCRIPTION*	**RECOMMENDED APPROACH**
3.1.18[a]	*Mobile devices that process, store, or*	P-Ensure an artifact is updated with carriers at least monthly (recommended)

	transmit CUI are identified.	
3.1.18[b]	*Mobile device connections are authorized.*	NCR
3.1.18[c]	*Mobile device connections are monitored and logged.*	P/T-Policy and notification to users should be documented and signed by every user (e.g., the AUP) and the carrier provides logs as requested or required.

ASSESSMENT METHODS AND CANDIDATE ARTIFACTS FOR REVIEW

Examine: [*SELECT FROM:* Access control policy; authorizations for mobile device connections to organizational systems; procedures addressing access control for mobile device usage (including restrictions); system design documentation; configuration management plan; system security plan; system audit logs and records; system configuration settings and associated documentation; other relevant documents or records].

Test: [*SELECT FROM:* Access control capability authorizing mobile device connections to organizational systems].

3.1.19. Encrypt CUI on mobile devices.

MINIMUM ANSWER: The good news is that all the major carriers provide DAR encryption. Mobile phones typically can secure DAR on the phone behind a passcode, PIN, or even biometric capability such as fingerprint or facial recognition; these are acceptable by government standards. Check service agreements or add to the company's existing plan.

MORE COMPLETE ANSWER: There are several companies that provide proprietary and hardened devices for corporate users. These include state of the art encryption standards and further hardened phone bodies to prevent physical exploits of lost or stolen mobile devices. *Expect these solutions to be costly.*

ASSESSMENT OBJECTIVE *Determine if:*		
SUB-CTRL	*DESCRIPTION*	**RECOMMENDED APPROACH**
3.1.19[a]	*Mobile devices and mobile computing platforms that process, store, or transmit CUI are identified.*	NCR

3.1.19[b]	Encryption is employed to protect CUI on identified mobile devices and mobile computing platforms.	NCR

ASSESSMENT METHODS AND CANDIDATE ARTIFACTS FOR REVIEW

Examine: [*SELECT FROM:* Access control policy; procedures addressing access control for mobile devices; system design documentation; system configuration settings and associated documentation; encryption mechanisms and associated configuration documentation; system security plan; system audit logs and records; other relevant documents or records].

Test: [*SELECT FROM:* Encryption mechanisms protecting confidentiality of information on mobile devices].

3.1.20 Verify and control/limit connections to and use of external systems.

MINIMUM ANSWER: This control requires that all external or third-party connections to the company's network be verified. This would typically take the form of accepting another company (or even State agencies') Authority to Operate (ATO). This could be as simple as a memorandum, for example, recognizing another company's self-assessment under NIST 800-171. It could also be accepted through a process known as **reciprocity**, of accepting an ATO based upon NIST 800-53—more typical of federal agencies. These are all legitimate means that are designed to ensure before a company allows another company to enter through its firewall (system security boundary) without some level of certainty that security was thoroughly considered. Before an external system or network is allowed unfettered access to the corporations' data, it is critical to identify the rules and restrictions for such access as part of this control.

As always, ensure procedures identify, and limit, such connections to only critical data feeds needed from third-parties to conduct formal business operations.

MORE COMPLETE ANSWER: This could include a request for ongoing scans of the external system or network every 30 days; this would be considered quite extreme, but dependent on data sensitivity. If sought, suggest that every six-month that the company receives copies of the anti-virus, anti-malware, and vulnerability patch scanning reports identifying current threats to the external system. This is designed to address inbound threats potentially and to enhance the company's overall security posture.

ASSESSMENT OBJECTIVE *Determine if:*		
SUB-CTRL	*DESCRIPTION*	**RECOMMENDED APPROACH**
3.1.20[a]	*Connections to external systems are identified.*	SSP-Should be identified in the architecture diagram
3.1.20[b]	*The use of external systems is identified.*	SSP-(See above)
3.1.20[c]	*Connections to external systems are verified.*	NCR
3.1.20[d]	*The use of external systems is verified.*	NCR
3.1.20[e]	*Connections to external systems are controlled/limited.*	NCR
3.1.20[f]	*The use of external systems is controlled/limited.*	NCR

ASSESSMENT METHODS AND CANDIDATE ARTIFACTS FOR REVIEW

Examine: [*SELECT FROM:* Access control policy; procedures addressing the use of external systems; terms and conditions for external systems; system security plan; list of applications accessible from external systems; system configuration settings and associated documentation; system connection or processing agreements; account management documents; other relevant documents or records].

Test: [*SELECT FROM:* Mechanisms implementing terms and conditions on use of external systems].

3.1.21 Limit use of organizational portable storage devices on external systems.

MINIMUM ANSWER: This is not only about the use of USB thumb drives (see Chapter on Media Protection (MP)), it is also about external drives attached to a workstation or laptop, locally. While thumb drives are more capable of introducing malware and viruses to an unprotected network, external drives pose a real threat to data removal and theft. The company policy should include an approval process to "attach" only company provided drives and highly discourage personal devices attached by employees. Technical support should include the active scanning for viruses and malware every time the portable device is attached to the network.

MORE COMPLETE ANSWER: As discussed in more detail below regarding the use of thumb drives, IT personnel could disable anyone from using the **registry**. Where the need for external drives is necessitated, this control can be further enhanced through auditing of all such attachments and provide pre-formatted reports for company leadership. Auditing, as described under the AU control, should include capturing this activity.

ASSESSMENT OBJECTIVE *Determine if:*		
SUB-CTRL	*DESCRIPTION*	**RECOMMENDED APPROACH**
3.1.21[a]	*The use of portable storage devices containing CUI on external systems is identified and documented.*	NCR
3.1.21[b]	*Limits on the use of portable storage devices containing CUI on external systems are defined.*	NCR
3.1.21[c]	*The use of portable storage devices containing CUI on external systems is limited as defined.*	NCR

ASSESSMENT METHODS AND CANDIDATE ARTIFACTS FOR REVIEW

Examine: [*SELECT FROM:* Access control policy; procedures addressing the use of external systems; system security plan; system configuration settings and associated documentation; system connection or processing agreements; account management documents; other relevant documents or records].

Test: [*SELECT FROM:* Mechanisms implementing restrictions on use of portable storage devices].

3.1.22 Control CUI posted or processed on publicly accessible systems.

MINIMUM ANSWER: This addresses the control of publicly accessible information most commonly on the company's **public-facing** website. There needs to be procedural guidance and direction about who can release (usually public affairs office, etc.) and post information (usually webmaster, etc.) to the website. This should include a review of such data by personnel specially trained to recognize CUI data. This may include information or data that discusses a company's current business relationship with the government, the activities it conducts, and the products and services it provides to both the public and private sector.

This should also address the regular review of publicly accessible data, and the procedure to describe the process to remove unauthorized data if discovered.

MORE COMPLETE ANSWER: This could use automated scans of keywords and phrases that may alert audit personnel during their regular auditing activities. See the Auditing Control (AU) chapter. While this is a static means to alert untrained IT personnel, it could supplement that inadvertent release does not occur. Additional oversight should always be based upon the sensitivity of the information handled not only to include CUI but Intellectual Property (IP) or other sensitive data, etc., that may harm the company if released into the public.

ASSESSMENT OBJECTIVE *Determine if:*		
SUB-CTRL	*DESCRIPTION*	**RECOMMENDED APPROACH**
3.1.22[a]	*Individuals authorized to post or process the information on publicly accessible systems are identified.*	NCR
3.1.22[b]	*Procedures to ensure CUI is not posted or processed on publicly accessible systems are identified.*	NCR
3.1.22[c]	*A review process is in place prior to posting of any content to publicly accessible systems.*	NCR
3.1.22[d]	*Content on publicly accessible systems is*	NCR

	reviewed to ensure that it does not include CUI.	
3.1.22[e]	Mechanisms are in place to remove and address improper posting of CUI.	NCR

ASSESSMENT METHODS AND CANDIDATE ARTIFACTS FOR REVIEW

Examine: [*SELECT FROM:* Access control policy; procedures addressing publicly accessible content; system security plan; list of users authorized to post publicly accessible content on organizational systems; training materials and/or records; records of publicly accessible information reviews; records of response to nonpublic information on public websites; system audit logs and records; security awareness training records; other relevant documents or records].

Test: [*SELECT FROM:* Mechanisms implementing management of publicly accessible content].

The decision process of how much encryption and added protection (such as hashing or emerging blockchain encryption technologies) should be based on the risk to the system.

Consider the risk and the damage to the company if the data, PERSONAL INFORMATION or not is compromised.

AWARENESS & TRAINING (AT)
A training program is a must

Awareness & Training is about an active cybersecurity training program for employees and a recurring education program that ensures their familiarity and compliance with protecting sensitive and CUI company data consistently. The websites (below) identify FREE government-sponsored sites a company can leverage without expending any of its resources. The three major training requirements that can be expected of most vendors supporting State government contract activities include:

1. **Cybersecurity Awareness Training.**
   https://securityawareness.usalearning.gov/cybersecurity/index.htm

2. **Insider Threat Training.**
   https://securityawareness.usalearning.gov/itawareness/index.htm
   (More discussion on the "Insider Threat" topic See Control 3.2.3).

3. **Privacy.**
   https://iatraining.disa.mil/eta/piiv2/launchPage.htm (This would correctly apply to any company that handles, processes, or maintains Personally Identifiable Information (PII) and Personal Health Information (PHI). The author expects that even though a company does not handle PII or PHI, the State government to make this a universal training requirement.)

Defense Security Service (DSS) Cybersecurity Awareness Site

Basic Security Requirements:

3.2.1 Ensure that managers, systems administrators, and users of organizational information systems are made aware of the security risks associated with their activities and of the applicable policies, standards, and procedures related to the security of organizational information systems.

MINIMUM ANSWER: Human beings are the weakest link in the cybersecurity "war." The greatest threat is from the employee who unwittingly selects a link that allows an intrusion into the corporate system, or worse, those who maliciously remove, modify, or delete sensitive CUI.

The answer should be documented regarding initial and annual refresher training requirements for everyone in the company; not average employees but must include senior managers and support subcontractors. Provide a sampling of select employees that have taken training, and ensuring it is current within the past year.

MORE COMPLETE ANSWER: A possible demonstration of the more-complete solution is within the policy specific direction to IT support personnel. There could be a system notification that allows them after notification, manually or by automated means, to suspend access to training is completed. Robust documentation is important specific to awareness training.

ASSESSMENT OBJECTIVE *Determine if:*		
SUB-CTRL	*DESCRIPTION*	RECOMMENDED APPROACH
3.2.1[a]	*Security risks associated with organizational activities involving CUI are identified.*	P-This would take the form of an initial and follow-on Risk Assessment (RA) for this control. Recommend an RA is conducted by the CIO, CISO, or like IT representative who conducts and review this review with senior leadership annually.
3.2.1[b]	*Policies, standards, and procedures related to the security of the system are identified.*	P- *"Policies, standards, and procedures related to the security of the system are identified AND DOCUMENTED annually in conjunction with a company RA [see above]."*
3.2.1[c]	*Managers, systems administrators, and users of the*	P-Add to current and future updates to cybersecurity awareness training specific to an RA.

		system are made aware of the security risks associated with their activities.	
3.2.1[d]		Managers, systems administrators, and users of the system are made aware of the applicable policies, standards, and procedures related to the security of the system.	P-Add to current and future updates to cybersecurity awareness training specific to an RA.

ASSESSMENT METHODS AND CANDIDATE ARTIFACTS FOR REVIEW

Examine: [*SELECT FROM:* Security awareness and training policy; procedures addressing security awareness training implementation; relevant codes of federal regulations; security awareness training curriculum; security awareness training materials; system security plan; training records; other relevant documents or records].

Test: [*SELECT FROM:* Mechanisms managing security awareness training; mechanisms managing role-based security training].

3.2.2 Ensure that organizational personnel is adequately trained to carry out their assigned information, security-related duties, and responsibilities.

MINIMUM ANSWER: This is required not only awareness training but also specialized training for privileged users. This is usually an Operating System (OS) training specific to the company's architecture. It is possible to have multiple OS's. Privileged users are only required to show, for example, some form of the training certificate, to meet this requirement. All IT personnel who have elevated privileges must have such training before they are authorized to execute their duties.

Additionally, if the company uses Microsoft ® or Linux ® Operating Systems, privileged users will have some level of certification to show familiarity with these programs. This could include major national certifications for these applications or basic familiarity courses from free training sites, for example, Khan Academy® (https://www.khanacademy.org/) or Udacity® (https://www.udacity.com/).

The government has not defined the level and type of training for this requirement. It requires privileged users to have an understanding and training certificate (with no specified time length) for the dominant Operating System (OS) the corporate IT infrastructure employs.

MORE COMPLETE ANSWER: If IT personnel have formal certification (such as from a Microsoft ® partner training program), these are ideal artifacts that should be part of the BOE.

ASSESSMENT OBJECTIVE *Determine if:*		
SUB-CTRL	*DESCRIPTION*	**RECOMMENDED APPROACH**
3.2.2[a]	*Information security-related duties, roles, and responsibilities are defined.*	NCR
3.2.2[b]	*Information security-related duties, roles, and responsibilities are assigned to designated personnel.*	NCR
3.2.2[c]	*Personnel is adequately trained to carry out their assigned information, security-related duties, roles, and responsibilities.*	NCR
ASSESSMENT METHODS AND CANDIDATE ARTIFACTS FOR REVIEW		

Examine: [*SELECT FROM:* Security awareness and training policy; procedures addressing security training implementation; codes of federal regulations; security training curriculum; security training materials; system security plan; training records; other relevant documents or records].

Test: [*SELECT FROM:* Mechanisms managing role-based security training; mechanisms managing security awareness training].

Derived Security Requirements:

3.2.3 Provide security awareness training on recognizing and reporting potential indicators of insider threat.

MINIMUM ANSWER: The DOD's Defense Security Service (DSS) in Quantico, VA, is the executive agent for insider threat activities. The DSS provides many training opportunities and toolkits on

Insider Threat. These are available from their agency website for free at http://www.dss.mil/it/index.html. This is an excellent resource to create an insider threat training program already developed for the company's use.

Document company minimum training requirements for both general and privileged users, such as watching select online instruction or computer-based training opportunities from DSS. Everyone in the company should participate and satisfactorily complete the training.

MORE COMPLETE ANSWER: More-complete proof of company compliance with this security control requirement might include guest speakers, or insider threat brown-bag events around lunchtime. Company training personnel should capture attendance records to include sign-in rosters. These could be used for annual training requirements specific to insider threat familiarity.

Also, recommend a **train-the-trainer program** where select individuals are trained by either DSS or other competent company that becomes corporate resources. These assigned individuals could provide both training and first-responder support as needed and be deployed to other company sites.

ASSESSMENT OBJECTIVE *Determine if:*		
SUB-CTRL	*DESCRIPTION*	**RECOMMENDED APPROACH**
3.2.3[a]	*Potential indicators associated with insider threats are identified.*	P-Identify this in association with a Risk Assessment (RA) as described in Control 3.2.2.
3.2.3[b]	*Security awareness training on recognizing and reporting potential indicators of insider threat is provided to managers and employees.*	NCR

ASSESSMENT METHODS AND CANDIDATE ARTIFACTS FOR REVIEW

Examine: [*SELECT FROM:* Security awareness and training policy; procedures addressing security awareness training implementation; security awareness training curriculum; security awareness training materials; insider threat policy and procedures; system security plan; other relevant documents or records].

Test: [*SELECT FROM:* Mechanisms managing insider threat training].

AUDIT AND ACCOUNTABILITY (AU)
System Logs and their Regular Review

The AU control is primarily about the ability of the system owner/company to monitor unauthorized access to the system through system logging functions of the Operating System and other network devices such as firewalls. A SA is typically assigned the duty to review log files; these may include both authorized and unauthorized access to the network, applications, databases, financial systems, etc. Most businesses will rely on manual review; however, some "smart" servers and firewalls can provide automated alerts to IT personnel of unauthorized use or intrusion. The key is to understand the auditing capabilities of the corporate system and be prepared to defend its capabilities and limitations if government representatives or third-party assessors request proof of control compliance.

```
   ..sion Detection System
.**] [1:1407:9] SNMP trap udp [**]
[Classification: Attempted Information Leak] [Priority: 2]
03/06-8:14:09.082119 192.168.1.167:1052 -> 172.30.128.27:162
UDP TTL:118 TOS:0x0 ID:29101 IpLen:20 DgmLen:87

Personal Firewall
3/6/2006 8:14:07 AM,"Rule ""Block Windows File Sharing"" blocked (192.168.1.54,
netbios-ssn(139)).","Rule ""Block Windows File Sharing"" blocked (192.168.1.54,
netbios-ssn(139)).  Inbound TCP connection.  Local address,service is
(KENT(172.30.128.27),netbios-ssn(139)).  Remote address,service is
(192.168.1.54,39922).  Process name is ""System""."

3/3/2006 9:04:04 AM,Firewall configuration updated: 398 rules.,Firewall configuration
updated: 398 rules.

Antivirus Software, Log 1
3/4/2006 9:33:50 AM,Definition File Download,KENT,userk,Definition downloader
3/4/2006 9:33:09 AM,AntiVirus Startup,KENT,userk,System
3/3/2006 3:56:46 PM,AntiVirus Shutdown,KENT,userk,System

Antivirus Software, Log 2
240203071234,16,3,7,KENT,userk,,,,,,,16777216,"Virus definitions are
current.",0,,0,,,,,0,,,,,,,,,,SAVPROD,{ xxxxxxxx-xxxx-xxxx-xxxx-xxxxxxxxxxxx },End
User,(IP)-192.168.1.121,,GROUP,0:0:0:0:0:0,9.0.0.338,,,,,,,,,,,,,

Antispyware Software
DSO Exploit: Data source object exploit (Registry change, nothing done)  HKEY_USERS\S-
1-5-19\Software\Microsoft\Windows\CurrentVersion\Internet Settings\Zones\0\1004!=W=>
```

Audit log type examples. The logs above are good examples of the system logs that should be reviewed regularly. These are the business's responsibility to monitor the network actively. Another term of high interest is **Continuous Monitoring (ConMon);** see the article in Appendix C discussing the importance of ConMon capabilities. ConMon can be accomplished by both manual and automated means, and auditing is a significant control family supporting the objectives of this cybersecurity principle.

ConMon activities are best described as the ability of the business to "continuously" monitor the state of its network within its defined security boundary. It should be a capability to determine, for example, who, when, and what are within the company's security boundary and any reporting requirements in the event of an intrusion. It will be based on log discovery of unauthorized activities. (SOURCE: *Guide to Computer Security Log Management*, NIST SP 800-92, September 2006, http://nvlpubs.nist.gov/nistpubs/Legacy/SP/nistspecialpublication800-92.pdf) .

For a better description of the purpose and components of Continuous Monitoring (ConMon) see Appendix D: ***Continuous Monitoring: A More Detailed Discussion.***

Basic Security Requirements:

3.3.1 Create, protect, and retain information system audit records to the extent needed to enable the monitoring, analysis, investigation, and reporting of unlawful, unauthorized, or inappropriate information system activity.
MINIMUM ANSWER: The critical part of this control is about audit record retention. The control defines the retention period as a vague capability to retain such records to the most significant "extent possible." The guidance should always be based on the sensitivity of the data. Another consideration should include the ability to provide forensic data to investigators to determine the intrusion over a period.

The historical OPM Breach occurred over several years until OPM even recognized multiple incidents. This included the exfiltration of millions of personnel and security background investigation files. OPM failures, while many, including poor audit processes and review, are a significant factor in the success of nation-state hackers. OPM's poor audit and retention processes made reconstructing critical events more than difficult for government forensics and associated criminal investigations.

The recommendation to small and medium businesses conducting US government contract activities would be at least one year and preferably two years of audit log retention. Companies should regularly discuss with government contract representatives its specified requirements. They should also visit the National Archives Record Agency (NARA) (www.nara.gov) for CUI data retention as part of an active audit program.

Businesses should balance operations (and long-term costs) with security (the ability to reconstruct an intrusion, to support law enforcement)

MORE COMPLETE ANSWER: A more exceptional ability to recognize breaches (events and incidents) could include a new internal process and assigned first-responders who would act upon these occurrences. This response team may have additional specialized training to include the use of select network analysis support tools to include packet inspection training using tools such as Wireshark ® (https://www.wireshark.org/).

ASSESSMENT OBJECTIVE *Determine if:*		
SUB-CTRL	*DESCRIPTION*	**RECOMMENDED APPROACH**
3.3.1[a]	*Audit logs needed (i.e., event types to be logged) to enable the monitoring, analysis, investigation, and reporting of unlawful or unauthorized system activity are specified.*	NCR
3.3.1[b]	*The content of audit records needed to support monitoring, analysis, investigation, and reporting of unlawful or unauthorized system activity is defined.*	NCR
3.3.1[c]	*Audit records are created (generated).*	NCR
3.3.1[d]	*Audit records, once created, contain the defined content.*	P - ("Defined content" is too vague. This should at a minimum be the login ID [the person], date-time

		stamp, IP address, MAC address, and all commands executed).
3.3.1[e]	*Retention requirements for audit records are defined.*	NCR – Refer to National Archives Record Agency (NARA) (www.nara.gov) for CUI data retention.
3.3.1[f]	*Audit records are retained as defined.*	NCR

ASSESSMENT METHODS AND CANDIDATE ARTIFACTS FOR REVIEW

Examine: [*SELECT FROM:* Audit and accountability policy; procedures addressing auditable events; system security plan; system design documentation; system configuration settings and associated documentation; procedures addressing control of audit records; procedures addressing audit record generation; system audit logs and records; system auditable events; system incident reports; other relevant documents or records].

Test: [*SELECT FROM:* Mechanisms implementing system audit logging].

3.3.2 Ensure that the actions of individual information system users can be uniquely traced to those users, so they can be held accountable for their actions.

MINIMUM ANSWER: This is about the capture of individual users as they access the system. Access logs should include, for example, user identification information, timestamps of all access, databases or applications accessed, and some failed login attempts. This control is designed for potential forensic reconstruction for either internal policy violations or external threat intrusions. Any policy considerations should include at least a weekly review, but any audit review periodicity should be based on the sensitivity and criticality of data to the business's overall mission.

MORE COMPLETE ANSWER: A more complete means to address this control is using automated alerts to crucial IT and management personnel. This could include capabilities from existing "smart" firewalls, or more advanced solutions may include a **Security Information & Event Management** (SIEM) solution. These are more complicated and expensive solutions, but current developments employing modern Artificial Intelligence and Machine Learning technologies to more proactively identify threats is evolving rapidly; these solutions should be less expensive and more comfortable to deploy within the next decade.

ASSESSMENT OBJECTIVE *Determine if:*		
SUB-CTRL	*DESCRIPTION*	**RECOMMENDED APPROACH**
3.3.2[a]	*The content of the audit records needed to support the ability to uniquely trace users to their actions is defined.*	NCR
3.3.2[b]	*Audit records, once created, contain the defined content.*	NCR

ASSESSMENT METHODS AND CANDIDATE ARTIFACTS FOR REVIEW

Examine: [*SELECT FROM:* Audit and accountability policy; procedures addressing audit records and event types; system security plan; system design documentation; system configuration settings and associated documentation; procedures addressing audit record generation; procedures addressing audit review, analysis, and reporting; reports of audit findings; system audit logs and records; system events; system incident reports; other relevant documents or records].

Test: [*SELECT FROM:* Mechanisms implementing system audit logging].

Derived Security Requirements:

3.3.3 Review and update audited events.

MINIMUM ANSWER: This is a similar requirement to other AU controls above to regularly review audit logs. ***We recommend at least weekly reviews***.

MORE COMPLETE ANSWER: To more completely address this control, IT personnel could categorize the log types being collected. These could include, for example, Operating System (OS) (network), application, firewall, database logs, etc.

ASSESSMENT OBJECTIVE *Determine if:*		
SUB-CTRL	*DESCRIPTION*	**RECOMMENDED APPROACH**
3.3.3[a]	*A process for determining when to review logged events is defined.*	NCR
3.3.3[b]	*Event types being logged are reviewed in accordance with*	*P- "Event types" could include failed logons, file deletions, modifications, or changes (especially in critical databases such as HR or finance).*

	the defined review process.		
3.3.3[c]	*Event types being logged are updated based on the review.*	P- (See Above)	

ASSESSMENT METHODS AND CANDIDATE ARTIFACTS FOR REVIEW

Examine: [*SELECT FROM:* Audit and accountability policy; procedures addressing audit records and event types; system security plan; list of organization-defined event types to be logged; reviewed and updated records of logged event types; system audit logs and records; system incident reports; other relevant documents or records].

Test: [*SELECT FROM:* Mechanisms supporting review and update of logged event types].

3.3.4 Alert in the event of an audit process failure.

MINIMUM ANSWER: This is an active ability developed within the company's audit technology that can alert personnel of an audit failure.

This could include local alarms, flashing lights, SMS, and email alerts to key company personnel. This will require SA and IT personnel to set policy settings to be established as part of the standard checks in support of the overall audit function and control. A description of the technical implementation and immediate actions to be taken by personnel should be identified. This should include the activation of the Incident Response (IR) Plan.

MORE COMPLETE ANSWER: Additional technical solutions could include supplementary systems to be monitored. This could include the state of all audit-capable devices and functions. This may also include a separate computer or a backup auditing server for the storage of logs not on the primary system; this would prevent intruders from deleting or changing logs to hide their presence in the network.

These solutions will ultimately add additional complexity and cost. Ensure any solution is supportable both financially and technically by company decision-makers. While to have greater security is an overall desire of the NIST 800-171 implementation, it should be balanced with a practical and measurable value-added approach to adding any new technologies. It should also be a further consideration that the incorporation of new technologies should address the impacts of added complexity and determining the ability of IT support personnel to maintain it.

ASSESSMENT OBJECTIVE *Determine if:*		
SUB-CTRL	***DESCRIPTION***	**RECOMMENDED APPROACH**
3.3.4[a]	*Personnel or roles to be alerted in the event of an audit logging process failure are identified.*	NCR
3.3.4[b]	*Types of audit logging process failures for which alert will be generated are defined.*	NCR
3.3.4[c]	*Identified personnel or roles are alerted in the event of an audit logging process failure.*	NCR

ASSESSMENT METHODS AND CANDIDATE ARTIFACTS FOR REVIEW

Examine: [*SELECT FROM:* Audit and accountability policy; procedures addressing response to audit logging processing failures; system design documentation; system security plan; system configuration settings and associated documentation; list of personnel to be notified in case of an audit logging processing failure; system incident reports; system audit logs and records; other relevant documents or records].

Test: [*SELECT FROM:* Mechanisms implementing system response to audit logging processing failures].

3.3.5 Correlate audit review, analysis, and reporting processes for investigation and response to indications of inappropriate, suspicious, or unusual activity.

MINIMUM ANSWER: This should identify the technical actions taken by authorized audit personnel to pursue when analyzing suspicious activity on the network.

It should also be tied to the IR Plan, and be tested at least annually. (See Control IR for further discussion of the **DOD Precedence Identification** example and determine actions based on the level of severity).

MORE COMPLETE ANSWER: See Control 3.3.2 for a more detailed discussion of employing a SIEM solution. In addition to manual analysis, the company could leverage the capabilities of newer threat identification technologies such as SIEM and "smart" Intrusion Detection and Prevention devices.

ASSESSMENT OBJECTIVE *Determine if:*		
SUB-CTRL	*DESCRIPTION*	RECOMMENDED APPROACH
3.3.5[a]	*Audit record review, analysis, and reporting processes for investigation and response to indications of unlawful, unauthorized, suspicious, or unusual activity are defined.*	NCR
3.3.5[b]	*Defined audit record review, analysis, and reporting processes are correlated.*	NCR

ASSESSMENT METHODS AND CANDIDATE ARTIFACTS FOR REVIEW

Examine: [*SELECT FROM:* Audit and accountability policy; procedures addressing audit record review, analysis, and reporting; system security plan; system design documentation; system configuration settings and associated documentation; procedures addressing investigation of and response to suspicious activities; system audit logs and records across different repositories; other relevant documents or records].

Test: [*SELECT FROM:* Mechanisms supporting analysis and correlation of audit records; mechanisms integrating audit review, analysis, and reporting].

3.3.6 Provide audit reduction and report generation to support on-demand analysis and reporting.

MINIMUM ANSWER: Audit reduction provides for "on-demand" audit review, analysis, and reporting requirements.

This should at least use manual methods to collect audits from across multiple audit logging devices to assist with potential forensic needs. Any procedural effort to support audit reduction most likely can use commercial support applications and scripts (small programs typically are explicitly written to the business's unique IT environment) that IT personnel should be able to assist in their identification, development, and procurement.

MORE COMPLETE ANSWER: IT personnel could identify more automated and integrated audit reduction solutions. Likely candidates could be "smart" firewalls or Security Information and Event Management (SIEM) solutions.

ASSESSMENT OBJECTIVE *Determine if:*		
SUB-CTRL	*DESCRIPTION*	**RECOMMENDED APPROACH**
3.3.6[a]	*An audit record reduction capability that supports on-demand analysis is provided.*	NCR (if required to automate then a POAM or Waiver may be necessary)
3.3.6[b]	*A report generation capability that supports on-demand reporting is provided.*	NCR (This could be as basic as a data-run to provide ad hoc reporting requests).

POTENTIAL ASSESSMENT METHODS AND CANDIDATE ARTIFACTS FOR REVIEW

Examine: [*SELECT FROM:* Audit and accountability policy; procedures are addressing audit record reduction and report generation; system design documentation; system security plan; system configuration settings and associated documentation; audit record reduction, review, analysis, and reporting tools; system audit logs and records; other relevant documents or records].

Test: [*SELECT FROM:* Audit record reduction and report generation capability].

3.3.7 Provide an information system capability that compares and synchronizes internal system clocks with an authoritative source to generate timestamps for audit records.

MINIMUM ANSWER: The most straightforward answer is to have IT personnel use the Network Time Protocol (NTP) on **NTP port 123** to provide US Naval Observatory timestamps as the standard for the network; this is considered the authoritative source. The system clocks of all processors (computers, firewalls, etc.) within the company should be set to the same time when first initialized by IT support staffs; this should be an explicit policy requirement.

It is suggested that SA personnel review and compare the external (NTP server time stamp) with internal system clocks. This can be used to identify log changes if synchronization is not the same from the external and internal clock settings. Log changes may be an indicator of unauthorized access and manipulation of log files by hackers.

MORE COMPLETE ANSWER: There are several automated programs that can be used, and good basic programmers within the company could write scripts (small pieces of executable code) to provide these comparisons more easily.

ASSESSMENT OBJECTIVE *Determine if:*		
SUB-CTRL	*DESCRIPTION*	**RECOMMENDED APPROACH**
3.3.7[a]	*Internal system clocks are used to generate timestamps for audit records.*	P-The control here is calling for relying on "internal" clocks; BE AWARE hackers can manipulate system clocks.
3.3.7[b]	*An authoritative source with which to compare and synchronize internal system clocks is specified.*	NCR
3.3.7[c]	*Internal system clocks used to generate timestamps for audit records are compared to and synchronized with the specified authoritative time source.*	NCR

POTENTIAL ASSESSMENT METHODS AND CANDIDATE ARTIFACTS FOR REVIEW

Examine: [*SELECT FROM:* Audit and accountability policy; procedures are addressing time stamp generation; system design documentation; system security plan; system configuration settings and associated documentation; system audit logs and records; other relevant documents or records].

Test: [*SELECT FROM:* Mechanisms implementing time stamp generation; mechanisms implementing internal information system clock synchronization].

3.3.8 Protect audit information and audit tools from unauthorized access, modification, and deletion.

MINIMUM ANSWER: This control requires greater protection of audit files and auditing tools from unauthorized users. These tools can be exploited by intruders to change log files or delete them entirely to hide their entry into the system. Password protect and limit use to only authorized personnel. Document this process accordingly.

MORE COMPLETE ANSWER: This information could be stored in some other server not part of the normal audit log capture area. Additionally, conduct regular backups to prevent intruders from manipulating logs; this will allow a means to compare changes, and identify potential incidents in the network for action by senior management or law enforcement.

ASSESSMENT OBJECTIVE *Determine if:*		
SUB-CTRL	*DESCRIPTION*	**RECOMMENDED APPROACH**
3.3.8[a]	*Audit information is protected from unauthorized access.*	NCR
3.3.8[b]	*Audit information is protected from unauthorized modification.*	NCR
3.3.8[c]	*Audit information is protected from unauthorized deletion.*	NCR
3.3.8[d]	*Audit logging tools are protected from unauthorized access.*	NCR
3.3.8[e]	*Audit logging tools are protected from unauthorized modification.*	NCR
3.3.8[f]	*Audit logging tools are protected from unauthorized deletion.*	NCR

ASSESSMENT METHODS AND CANDIDATE ARTIFACTS FOR REVIEW

Examine: [*SELECT FROM:* Audit and accountability policy; access control policy and procedures; procedures addressing protection of audit information; system security plan; system design documentation; system configuration settings and associated documentation, system audit logs, and records; audit logging tools; other relevant documents or records].

Test: [*SELECT FROM:* Mechanisms implementing audit information protection].

3.3.9 Limit management of audit functionality to a subset of privileged users.

MINIMUM ANSWER: See Control 3.3.8 for reducing the numbers of personnel with access to audit logs and functions. Maintaining a roster of personnel with appropriate user agreements can afford the ability to limit personnel as well as provide value in any future forensic activities required.

MORE COMPLETE ANSWER: There are several products such as CyberArk ® that could be used to manage and monitor privileged user access to audit information. This product will be a relatively expensive solution for small and some medium-sized businesses.

ASSESSMENT OBJECTIVE *Determine if:*		
SUB-CTRL	*DESCRIPTION*	**RECOMMENDED APPROACH**
3.3.9[a]	*A subset of privileged users granted access to manage audit logging functionality is defined.*	NCR
3.3.9[b]	*Management of audit logging functionality is limited to the defined subset of privileged users.*	NCR

POTENTIAL ASSESSMENT METHODS AND CANDIDATE ARTIFACTS FOR REVIEW

Examine: [*SELECT FROM:* Audit and accountability policy; access control policy and procedures; procedures addressing protection of audit information; system security plan; system design documentation; system configuration settings and associated documentation; access authorizations; system-generated list of privileged users with access to management of audit logging functionality; access control list; system audit logs and records; other relevant documents or records].

Test: [*SELECT FROM:* Mechanisms managing access to audit logging functionality].

CONFIGURATION MANAGEMENT (CM)
The True Foundation of Cybersecurity

The real importance of Configuration Management is it is, in fact, the "opposite side of the same coin" called cybersecurity. CM is used to track and confirm changes to the system's baseline; this could be changed in hardware, firmware, and software that would alert IT professionals to unauthorized changes to the IT environment. CM is used to confirm and ensure programmatic controls prevent changes that have not been adequately tested or approved.

CM requires establishing baselines for tracking, controlling, and managing a business's internal IT infrastructure specific to NIST 800-171. Companies with an effective CM process need to consider information security implications for the development and operation of information systems. This will include the active management of changes to company hardware, software, and documentation.

The active CM of information systems requires the integration of the management of secure configurations into the CM process. If good CM exists as a well-defined "change" process, the protection of the IT environment is more assured. This should be considered as the second most important security control. It is suggested that both management and IT personnel have adequate knowledge and training to maintain this process since it is so integral to good programmatic and cybersecurity practice.

Basic Security Requirements:

3.4.1 Establish and maintain baseline configurations and inventories of organizational information systems (including hardware, software, firmware, and documentation) throughout the respective system development life cycles.
MINIMUM ANSWER: This control can be best met by hardware, software, and firmware (should be combined with hardware) listings; these are the classic artifacts required for any system. Updating these documents as changes to the IT architecture is both a critical IT and logistics' functions. Ensure these staffs are well-coordinated about system changes. *This should be included in the System Security Plan (SSP).*

Also, NIST 800-171 requires document control of all reports, documents, manuals, etc. The currency of all related documents should be managed in a centralized repository.

Where documents may be sensitive, such as describing existing weaknesses or vulnerabilities of the IT infrastructure, these documents should have a higher level of control. The rationale for greater control of such documents is if these documents were "found" in the public, hackers, or Advanced Persistent Threats (i.e., adversarial nation-states) could use to this information to conduct exploits. Vulnerabilities about company systems should be marked and controlled at least at the CUI level.

MORE COMPLETE ANSWER: Suggested better approaches to exercising suitable **version control** activities would be using a shared network drive, or a more advanced solution could use Microsoft ® SharePoint ®. An active version control tool should only allow authorized personnel to make changes to critical documents and system changes and their associated **versioning**— significant changes within the IT architecture, for example, from version 2.0 to 3.0. This should also maintain audit records of who and when a file is accessed and modified.

ASSESSMENT OBJECTIVE *Determine if:*		
SUB-CTRL	*DESCRIPTION*	**RECOMMENDED APPROACH**
3.4.1[a]	*A baseline configuration is established.*	NCR(SSP) - The SSP is the defined artifact to capture such information
3.4.1[b]	*The baseline configuration includes hardware, software, firmware, and documentation.*	NCR(SSP)
3.4.1[c]	*The baseline configuration is maintained (reviewed and updated) throughout the system development life cycle.*	P-Need to define and update as changes in configuration occur. Who or what body updates and maintains the "baseline" specific to the SSP
3.4.1[d]	*A system inventory is established.*	NCR(SSP)

3.4.1[e]	The system inventory includes hardware, software, firmware, and documentation.	NCR(SSP)
3.4.1[f]	The inventory is maintained (reviewed and updated) throughout the system development life cycle.	P-See Sub-control 3.4.1[c]

ASSESSMENT METHODS AND CANDIDATE ARTIFACTS FOR REVIEW

Examine: [SELECT FROM: Configuration management policy; procedures addressing the baseline configuration of the system; procedures addressing system inventory; system security plan; configuration management plan; system inventory records; inventory review and update records; enterprise architecture documentation; system design documentation; system architecture and configuration documentation; system configuration settings and associated documentation; change control records; system component installation records; system component removal records; other relevant documents or records].

Test: [SELECT FROM: Organizational processes for managing baseline configurations; mechanisms supporting configuration control of the baseline configuration; organizational processes for developing and documenting an inventory of system components; organizational processes for updating an inventory of system components; mechanisms supporting or implementing the system inventory; mechanisms implementing updating of the system inventory].

3.4.2 Establish and enforce security configuration settings for information technology products employed in organizational information systems.

MINIMUM/MORE COMPLETE ANSWER: There should be an identification of any security configuration settings in a business's procedural documents. This would include technical policy settings, for example, the number of failed logins, minimum password length, mandatory logoff settings, etc. These settings should be identified by a company's Operating System, software application, or program.

ASSESSMENT OBJECTIVE Determine if:		
SUB-CTRL	**DESCRIPTION**	**RECOMMENDED APPROACH**
3.4.2[a]	Security configuration settings for information	P- "Security configuration settings for information technology products employed in the system are established and included in the baseline configuration."

		technology products employed in the system are established and included in the baseline configuration.	
3.4.2[b]	Security configuration settings for information technology products employed in the system are enforced.	P- "Security configuration settings for information technology products employed in the system are enforced."	

Examine: [SELECT FROM: Configuration management policy; baseline configuration; procedures addressing configuration settings for the system; configuration management plan; system security plan; system design documentation; system configuration settings and associated documentation; security configuration checklists; evidence supporting approved deviations from established configuration settings; change control records; system audit logs and records; other relevant documents or records].

Test: [SELECT FROM: Organizational processes for managing configuration settings; mechanisms that implement, monitor, and/or control system configuration settings; mechanisms that identify and/or document deviations from established configuration settings; processes for managing baseline configurations; mechanisms supporting configuration control of baseline configurations].

Derived Security Requirements:

3.4.3 Track, review, approve/disapprove, and audit changes to information systems.

MINIMUM ANSWER: This control addresses a defined corporate change *process*. This should be able to add or remove IT components within the network and provide needed currency regarding the state of the network. This should not be a purely IT staff function. If the firm can afford additional infrastructure personnel, it should assign a configuration manager; this person would administer the CM process.

MORE COMPLETE ANSWER: This could use Commercial Off the Shelf Technologies (COTS) that could be used to establish a more sophisticated CM database. This could also afford a more capable audit ability to prevent unauthorized changes.

ASSESSMENT OBJECTIVE *Determine if:*		
SUB-CTRL	*DESCRIPTION*	RECOMMENDED APPROACH

3.4.3[a]	Changes to the system are tracked.	NCR
3.4.3[b]	Changes to the system are reviewed.	NCR
3.4.3[c]	Changes to the system are approved or disapproved.	NCR
3.4.3[d]	Changes to the system are logged.	NCR

ASSESSMENT METHODS AND CANDIDATE ARTIFACTS FOR REVIEW

Examine: [*SELECT FROM:* Configuration management policy; procedures addressing system configuration change control; configuration management plan; system architecture and configuration documentation; system security plan; change control records; system audit logs and records; change control audit and review reports; agenda/minutes from configuration change control oversight meetings; other relevant documents or records].

Test: [*SELECT FROM:* Organizational processes for configuration change control; mechanisms that implement configuration change control].

3.4.4 Analyze the security impact of changes prior to implementation.

MINIMUM ANSWER: Under NIST's risk management process, it requires that any changes to the baseline necessitate some level of technical analysis. This analysis is described as a **Security Impact Analysis (SIA),** and it is looking for any positive or negative changes that are considered **security-relevant**.

This analysis should look at any change to the architecture, be it changes in hardware, software, firmware, or architecture. This should be described in the corporate CM process and could be as essential as a write-up from a member of the IT team, for example, that the change will or will not have a security impact, and it may or may not be security-relevant.

If the change introduces a "negative" impact, such as eliminating backup capabilities or introducing currently unsupportable software (possibly due to funding constraints**), *it is the responsibility of the company to reinitiate the NIST 800-171 process in-full and advise the government of the rationale for the change.***

See CM control 3.4.4 for a detailed Decision-tree.

MORE COMPLETE ANSWER: A more-complete solution to this control would include, for example, the addition of a new software product that supports vulnerability scans using corporate anti-virus and malware applications or software products. Attach these reports as part of the record.

In the case of hardware updates, the company could demonstrate its SCRM process by attaching proof that the manufacturer is an authorized vendor approved by the government. Access to federal government Approved Products List (APL) may require the State AG Office to provide a means to access this resource.[11] The positive review of these databases will demonstrate the proper level of due diligence for any current or future Authorization to Operate (ATO).

3.4.5 Define, document, approve, and enforce physical and logical access restrictions associated with changes to the information system.

MINIMUM/MORE COMPLETE ANSWER: "Access restrictions" are aligned with the earlier discussed AC controls. As part of a corporate CM policy, any changes to the IT baseline needs to be captured within a formal process approved by that process and documented.

Documentation is typically maintained in a CM database, and more specifically, it would require the update of any hardware or software lists. Proof of compliance would be the production of updated listings that are maintained by the CM database. This should include the updating of any network diagrams describing in a graphic form a description of the corporate network; these are all explicit requirements under NIST 800-171. These artifacts should also be included in the **SSP**.

ASSESSMENT OBJECTIVE *Determine if:*		
SUB-CTRL	*DESCRIPTION*	RECOMMENDED APPROACH
3.4.5[a]	*Physical access restrictions associated with changes to the system are defined.*	NCR
3.4.5[b]	*Physical access restrictions associated with changes to the system are documented.*	NCR
3.4.5[c]	*Physical access restrictions associated*	NCR

---

[11] At this time, it is not required under the CCPA, but provides a potential future resource for consideration.

	with changes to the system are approved.	
3.4.5[d]	*Physical access restrictions associated with changes to the system are enforced.*	NCR
3.4.5[e]	*Logical access restrictions associated with changes to the system are defined.*	NCR- ("Logical access" is described under Access Control is full).
3.4.5[f]	*Logical access restrictions associated with changes to the system are documented.*	NCR
3.4.5[g]	*Logical access restrictions associated with changes to the system are approved.*	NCR
3.4.5[h]	*Logical access restrictions associated with changes to the system are enforced.*	NCR

ASSESSMENT METHODS AND CANDIDATE ARTIFACTS FOR REVIEW

Examine: [*SELECT FROM:* Configuration management policy; procedures addressing access restrictions for changes to the system; system security plan; configuration management plan; system design documentation; system architecture and configuration documentation; system configuration settings and associated documentation; logical access approvals; physical access approvals; access credentials; change control records; system audit logs and records; other relevant documents or records].

Test: [*SELECT FROM:* Organizational processes for managing access restrictions associated with changes to the system; mechanisms supporting, implementing, and enforcing access restrictions associated with changes to the system].

3.4.6 Employ the principle of least functionality by configuring the information system to provide only essential capabilities.

MINIMUM ANSWER: Parts of the government have defined the use, for example, of File Transfer Protocol (FTP), Bluetooth, or peer-to-peer networking as insecure protocols. These protocols are unauthorized within many State government environments, and companies seeking NIST 800-171 approval are best to follow this direction as well. Any written procedure should attempt to at least annually reassess whether a determination of the security of all functions, ports, protocols, or services are still correct.

MORE COMPLETE ANSWER: The use of automated network packet tools is recommended to conduct such reassessments. Ensure that IT personnel have the right experience and skill to provide a proper analysis of this control requirement.

ASSESSMENT OBJECTIVE *Determine if:*		
SUB-CTRL	*DESCRIPTION*	**RECOMMENDED APPROACH**
3.4.6[a]	*Essential system capabilities are defined based on the principle of least functionality.*	NCR- (See earlier discussion regarding conducting an initial and annual Risk Assessment (RA))
3.4.6[b]	*The system is configured to provide only the defined essential capabilities.*	NCR

ASSESSMENT METHODS AND CANDIDATE ARTIFACTS FOR REVIEW

Examine: [*SELECT FROM:* Configuration management policy; configuration management plan; procedures addressing least functionality in the system; system security plan; system design documentation; system configuration settings and associated documentation; security configuration checklists; other relevant documents or records].

Test: [*SELECT FROM:* Organizational processes prohibiting or restricting functions, ports, protocols, or services; mechanisms implementing restrictions or prohibition of functions, ports, protocols, or services].

3.4.7 Restrict, disable, and prevent the use of nonessential programs, functions, ports, protocols, and services.

MINIMUM ANSWER: Nonessential programs, functions, ports, and protocols are prime attack avenues for would-be hackers. Any programs that are not used for the conduct of business operations should be removed. Where that is not possible, these programs should be blacklisted to run in the company's IT environment. (See 3.4.8. below).

Regarding ports and protocols, this will require IT staff direct involvement in the decision-making process. Specific ports are typically needed for any 21st Century company's daily operation. For example, ports 80, 8080, and 443 are used to send HTTP (web traffic); these ports will typically be required to be active.

Port Number	Application Supported
20	File Transport Protocol (FTP) Data
23	Telnet
25	Simple Mail Transfer Protocol (SMTP)
80, 8080, 443	Hypertext Transport Protocol (HTTP) → WWW
110	Post Office Protocol version 3 (POP3)

Standard Ports and Their Associated Protocols

For those ports and protocols that are not required, they should be closed by designated IT personnel. This prevents hackers from exploiting open entries into the corporate infrastructure. Ensure a copy of all open and closed ports is readily available to government representatives for review as part of the NIST 800-171 requirements.

MORE COMPLETE ANSWER: The business could employ tools that check for unused and open ports. This could include a regular reassessment of whether ports need to remain active. As mentioned earlier, products such as Wireshark ® could be used as a low-cost solution to conduct any reassessment of the corporate infrastructure.

ASSESSMENT OBJECTIVE *Determine if:*		
SUB-CTRL	*DESCRIPTION*	**RECOMMENDED APPROACH**
3.4.7[a]	*Essential programs are defined.*	NCR (Always consult with Contract Office to determine any specified unauthorized programs, for example, "hacker tools," etc.
3.4.7[b]	*The use of nonessential programs is defined.*	NCR
3.4.7[c]	*The use of nonessential programs is restricted, disabled, or prevented as defined.*	NCR
3.4.7[d]	*Essential functions are defined.*	NCR (artifact would include all "whitelisted" applications and functions)

3.4.7[e]	*The use of nonessential functions is defined.*	NCR
3.4.7[f]	*The use of nonessential functions is restricted, disabled, or prevented as defined.*	NCR
3.4.7[g]	*Essential ports are defined.*	NCR (Coordinate with Contract office at least annually regarding any updates to unauthorized ports).
3.4.7[h]	*The use of nonessential ports is defined.*	NCR
3.4.7[i]	*The use of nonessential ports is restricted, disabled, or prevented as defined.*	NCR
3.4.7[j]	*Essential protocols are defined.*	NCR (Same as 3.4.7[g])
3.4.7[k]	*The use of nonessential protocols is defined.*	NCR
3.4.7[l]	*The use of nonessential protocols is restricted, disabled, or prevented as defined.*	NCR
3.4.7[m]	*Essential services are defined.*	NCR (Same as 3.4.7[g])
3.4.7[n]	*The use of nonessential services is defined.*	NCR
3.4.7[o]	*The use of nonessential*	NCR

services is restricted, disabled, or prevented as defined.	

ASSESSMENT METHODS AND CANDIDATE ARTIFACTS FOR REVIEW

Examine: [*SELECT FROM:* Configuration management policy; procedures addressing least functionality in the system; configuration management plan; system security plan; system design documentation; security configuration checklists; system configuration settings and associated documentation; specifications for preventing software program execution; documented reviews of programs, functions, ports, protocols, and/or services; change control records; system audit logs and records; other relevant documents or records].

Test: [*SELECT FROM:* Organizational processes for reviewing and disabling nonessential programs, functions, ports, protocols, or services; mechanisms implementing review and handling of nonessential programs, functions, ports, protocols, or services; organizational processes preventing program execution on the system; organizational processes for software program usage and restrictions; mechanisms supporting or implementing software program usage and restrictions; mechanisms preventing program execution on the system].

3.4.8 Apply deny-by-exception (blacklist) policy to prevent the use of unauthorized software or deny all, permit-by-exception (whitelisting) policy to allow the execution of authorized software.

MINIMUM/MORE COMPLETE ANSWER: The company should employ **blacklisting** or **whitelisting,** (See Control 3.14.2 for more information), to prohibit the execution of unauthorized software programs or applications within the information system. A copy of the current listing should be part of the formal Body of Evidence (BOE).

ASSESSMENT OBJECTIVE *Determine if:*		
SUB-CTRL	*DESCRIPTION*	**RECOMMENDED APPROACH**
3.4.8[a]	*A policy specifying whether whitelisting or blacklisting is to be implemented is specified.*	NCR
3.4.8[b]	*The software allowed to execute under whitelisting or denied use under blacklisting is specified.*	NCR
3.4.8[c]	*Whitelisting to allow the execution of authorized software or blacklisting to prevent the use of*	NCR

	unauthorized software is implemented as specified.	

ASSESSMENT METHODS AND CANDIDATE ARTIFACTS FOR REVIEW

Examine: [*SELECT FROM:* Configuration management policy; procedures addressing least functionality in the system; system security plan; configuration management plan; system design documentation; system configuration settings and associated documentation; list of software programs not authorized to execute on the system; list of software programs authorized to execute on the system; security configuration checklists; review and update records associated with list of authorized or unauthorized software programs; change control records; system audit logs and records; other relevant documents or records].

Test: [*SELECT FROM:* Organizational process for identifying, reviewing, and updating programs authorized or not authorized to execute on the system; process for implementing blacklisting or whitelisting; mechanisms supporting or implementing blacklisting or whitelisting].

3.4.9 Control and monitor user-installed software.

MINIMUM ANSWER: The policy should always be that only authorized administrators, such as designated SA's and senior help desk personnel, be allowed to add or delete the software from user computers.

There should also be a defined process to request specialized software be added for unique users. These may include finance personnel, architects, statisticians, etc. that require specialized stand-alone software that may or may not connect to the Internet.

MORE COMPLETE ANSWER: This could include as part of the company's normal audit process the review of whether personnel is adding software and bypassing security measures (such as getting passwords from IT authorized individuals). This may also be addressed in the AUP and supported by appropriate HR activities that can be pursued against individuals of any such violations.

ASSESSMENT OBJECTIVE *Determine if:*		
SUB-CTRL	*DESCRIPTION*	**RECOMMENDED APPROACH**
3.4.9[a]	*A policy for controlling the installation of software by users is established.*	NCR
3.4.9[b]	*Installation of software by users is controlled based on the established policy.*	NCR
3.4.9[c]	*Installation of software by users is monitored.*	NCR

ASSESSMENT METHODS AND CANDIDATE ARTIFACTS FOR REVIEW

Examine: [*SELECT FROM:* Configuration management policy; procedures addressing user-installed software; configuration management plan; system security plan; system design documentation; system configuration settings and associated documentation; list of rules governing user-installed software; system monitoring records; system audit logs and records; continuous monitoring strategy; other relevant documents or records].

Test: [*SELECT FROM:* Organizational processes governing user-installed software on the system; mechanisms enforcing rules or methods for governing the installation of software by users; mechanisms monitoring policy compliance].

IDENTIFICATION AND AUTHENTICATION (IA)
Why two-factor authentication is so important?

The 2015 Office of Personnel Management (OPM) breach could have been prevented if this control family was adequately implemented and enforced. The one "positive" effect that the OPM breach caused for federal agencies was the requirement from Congress that these requirements became mandatory. Congress's focus on the use of Two-Factor Authentication (2FA) and Multi-Factor Authentication (MFA) has provided useful results for the federal government and impetus for more stringent cybersecurity measures beyond the government's IT boundaries.

While some businesses will be afforded, for example, Common Access Cards (CAC) or Personal Identity Verification (PIV) cards to accomplish 2FA between the company and the government, most will not be authorized such access. Implementation will require various levels of investment, and the use of 2FA devices, or also called "tokens." This too, will require additional financial costs and technical integration challenges for the average business.

For many small businesses, this will also require some sizeable investments on the part of the company and a clear commitment to working with the government. Solutions could include, for example, RSA® tokens—these are small devices that regularly rotate a security variable (a key) that a user enters in addition to a password or Personal Identification Number (PIN). This solution affords one potential solution to businesses to meet the 2FA requirement.

⚖ *According to The House Committee on Oversight and Government Reform report on September 7th, 2016, OPM's leadership failed to "implement basic cyber hygiene, such as maintaining current authorities to operate <u>and employing strong multi-factor authentication</u>, despite years of warning from the Inspector General... tools were available that could have prevented the breaches..."* (SOURCE: https://oversight.house.gov/wp-content/uploads/2016/09/The-OPM-Data-Breach-How-the-Government-Jeopardized-Our-

The best approaches will require useful market surveys of the available resources and be mindful that two-factor does not need to be a card or token solution. Other options would include biometrics (fingerprints, facial recognition, etc.) or Short Message Service (SMS) 2FA solution as used by Amazon® to verify its customers. They use a Two-Step verification process that provides a "verification code sent to the customer's personal cell phone or home phone to verify their identity.

Be prepared to do serious "homework" on these controls and research all potential solutions. Once this control is resolved, the company will be in a better position not just with the government but have serious answers that will ensure the protection of its sensitive data.

Basic Security Requirements:

3.5.1 Identify information system users, processes acting on behalf of users, or devices.

MINIMUM/MORE COMPLETE ANSWER: This control should identify/reference current business procedures as outlined in the **AU** control above. It should address that audit is used to identify system users, the processes (applications) and the devices (computers) accessed.

ASSESSMENT OBJECTIVE *Determine if:*		
SUB-CTRL	*DESCRIPTION*	**RECOMMENDED APPROACH**
3.5.1[a]	*System users are identified.*	NCR
3.5.1[b]	*Processes acting on behalf of users are identified.*	NCR (through audit log collection)
3.5.1[c]	*Devices accessing the system are identified.*	NCR
ASSESSMENT METHODS AND CANDIDATE ARTIFACTS FOR REVIEW Examine: [*SELECT FROM:* Identification and authentication policy; procedures addressing user identification and authentication; system security plan, system design documentation; system configuration settings and associated documentation; system audit logs and records; list of system accounts; other relevant documents or records]. Test: [*SELECT FROM:* Organizational processes for uniquely identifying and authenticating users; mechanisms supporting or implementing identification and authentication capability].		

3.5.2 Authenticate (or verify) the identities of those users, processes, or devices, as a prerequisite to allowing access to organizational information systems.

MINIMUM ANSWER: While primary logon and password information could be used, Control 3.5.3 below, requires Multifactor or Two-factor Authentication (2FA). The government requires 2FA, and NIST 800-171 requires it as well.

**Remember, if the company is not immediately prepared to execute a 2FA solution, *a POAM is required*.

MORE COMPLETE ANSWER: The better answer is the employment of some form of 2FA. It could be a **hard token** solution such as a CAC or PIV card. The other option would include such virtual solutions that would use email or SMS messaging like Google ® or Amazon ® to provide 2FA; this **soft token** solution is typically more natural and less expensive to deploy. It can be more easily deployed to meet NIST 800-171 requirement.

ASSESSMENT OBJECTIVE *Determine if:*		
SUB-CTRL	*DESCRIPTION*	**RECOMMENDED APPROACH**
3.5.2[a]	*The identity of each user is authenticated or verified as a prerequisite to system access.*	NCR
3.5.2[b]	*The identity of each process acting on behalf of a user is authenticated or verified as a prerequisite to system access.*	NCR
3.5.2[c]	*The identity of each device accessing or connecting to the system is authenticated or verified as a*	P/T/PO/W- This will require policy and potential technical control updates where, for example, servers are authenticating to other servers securely. This may require a POAM or waiver in certain time-restricted circumstances.

	prerequisite to system access.	

ASSESSMENT METHODS AND CANDIDATE ARTIFACTS FOR REVIEW

Examine: [*SELECT FROM:* Identification and authentication policy; system security plan; procedures addressing authenticator management; procedures addressing user identification and authentication; system design documentation; list of system authenticator types; system configuration settings and associated documentation; change control records associated with managing system authenticators; system audit logs and records; other relevant documents or records].

Test: [*SELECT FROM:* Mechanisms supporting or implementing authenticator management capability].

Derived Security Requirements:

3.5.3 Use multifactor authentication for local and network access to privileged accounts and for network access to non-privileged accounts.

MINIMUM ANSWER: See Control 3.5.2 above. Ensure the requirement for MFA or 2FA is part of the company's cybersecurity policy/procedure.

MORE COMPLETE ANSWER: (See Control 3.5.2 for suggested approaches).

ASSESSMENT OBJECTIVE *Determine if:*		
SUB-CTRL	**DESCRIPTION**	**RECOMMENDED APPROACH**
3.5.3[a]	*Privileged accounts are identified.*	NCR
3.5.3[b]	*Multifactor authentication is implemented for local access to privileged accounts.*	NCR (At least two-factor authentication; Windows 10® allows for biometric facial recognition—a potential small architecture solution for many)
3.5.3[c]	*Multifactor authentication is implemented for network access to privileged accounts.*	NCR
3.5.3[d]	*Multifactor authentication is implemented for network access to non-privileged accounts.*	NCR

3.5.4 Employ replay-resistant authentication mechanisms for network access to privileged and nonprivileged accounts.

MINIMUM ANSWER: This control requires replay-resistant technologies to prevent replay attacks. **Replay attacks** are also known as a **playback attack**. This is an attack where the hacker captures legitimate traffic from an authorized user, and presumably a positively identified network user, and uses it to gain unauthorized access to a network. This is also considered a form of a **Man-in-the-Middle** type attack.

The most natural solution to resolving this control is to have company IT personnel disable **Secure Socket Layer (SSL)**—which the government no longer authorizes. Businesses should use the **Transport Layer Security (TLS) 2.0** or higher; it as a required government standard.

If the business needs to continue the use of SSL to maintain connectivity with, for example, external or third-party data providers, a POAM is required. Efforts should be made to discuss with these data providers when they will no longer be using SSL. This discussion should begin as soon as possible to advise the government through a POAM that demonstrates the company is conducting its proper due diligence to protect its CUI.

MORE COMPLETE ANSWER: A potentially expensive solution could include the addition of a **SIEM** solution. There are many major IT network providers that have added artificial intelligence capabilities to detect this type of attack better; identify any solution carefully.

3.5.5 Prevent reuse of identifiers for a defined period.

MINIMUM ANSWER: This IA control directs that "individual, group, role, or device identifiers" from being reused. This should be included as part of any written procedure and defined in system policies to prevent identifiers from being reused. This could include email address names (individual), administrator accounts (group), or device identifiers such as "finan_db" designating a high-value target such as a "financial database" (device).

The reason for this control is to prevent intruders who have gained information about such identifiers having less of a capability to use this information for an exploit of the business. This will help better thwart hacker's intelligence collection and analysis of a company's internal network. This control is designed to prevent intruders' abilities to gain access to corporate systems and their resident CUI repositories.

MORE COMPLETE ANSWER: Reuse of individual identifiers should be discouraged, for example, in the case of a returning employee. This is an essential suggestion: 'John.Smith@cui-company.com' could be varied examples, 'John.H.Smith2@cui-company.com.

ASSESSMENT OBJECTIVE *Determine if:*		
SUB-CTRL	*DESCRIPTION*	**RECOMMENDED APPROACH**
3.5.5[a]	*A period within which identifiers cannot be reused is defined.*	NCR
3.5.5[b]	*Reuse of identifiers is prevented within the defined period.*	NCR

ASSESSMENT METHODS AND CANDIDATE ARTIFACTS FOR REVIEW

Examine: [*SELECT FROM:* Identification and authentication policy; procedures addressing identifier management; procedures addressing account management; system security plan; system design documentation; system configuration settings and associated documentation; list of system accounts; list of identifiers generated from physical access control devices; other relevant documents or records].

Test: [*SELECT FROM:* Mechanisms supporting or implementing identifier management].

3.5.6 Disable identifiers after a defined period of inactivity.

MINIMUM/MORE COMPLETE ANSWER: This requires that after a defined time-out setting, the system terminates its connection. The recommendation is 30 minutes maximum, but as mentioned earlier, the time-out should always be based on the data sensitivity.

ASSESSMENT OBJECTIVE *Determine if:*		
SUB-CTRL	*DESCRIPTION*	**RECOMMENDED APPROACH**
3.5.6[a]	*A period of inactivity after which an identifier is disabled is defined.*	NCR
3.5.6[b]	*Identifiers are disabled after the defined period of inactivity.*	NCR

3.5.7 Enforce a minimum password complexity and change of characters when new passwords are created.

MINIMUM ANSWER: If using passwords for authentication purposes, the expectation is that a POAM has been developed until such time a 2FA or MFA solution is in place. The standard complexity is supposed to be at least 15 characters that include at least two or more alpha, numeric, and special characters to reduce the likelihood of compromise.

MORE COMPLETE ANSWER: Increased length and variability can be enforced by automated policy settings of the network. Another suggestion is to use passphrases. These can be harder to "crack" by standard hacking tools and are typically more natural for users to memorize.

ASSESSMENT OBJECTIVE *Determine if:*

SUB-CTRL	DESCRIPTION	RECOMMENDED APPROACH
3.5.7[a]	Password complexity requirements are defined.	NCR
3.5.7[b]	Password change of character requirements is defined.	NCR
3.5.7[c]	Minimum password complexity requirements, as defined, are enforced when new passwords are created.	NCR (Consult with Contract Office specific to DOD's 15-character alpha-numeric requirement)
3.5.7[d]	Minimum password change of character requirements as defined is enforced when new passwords are created.	NCR

The best solutions are still either 2FA or MFA

The factors:

- **1-FACTOR: Something you know (e.g., password/PIN)**
- **2-FACTOR: Something you have (e.g., cryptographic identification device, token)**
- **MULTI-FACTOR: Something you are (e.g., biometric: fingerprint, iris, etc.)**

3.5.8 Prohibit password reuse for a specified number of generations.

MINIMUM ANSWER: This is usually set by policy and the designated SA's that limit the number of times a password can be reused; *passwords within most parts of the government are required to be changed every 90 days.* This function should be automated by authorized IT personnel. Suggested reuse of a prior password should be at least ten or greater

MORE COMPLETE ANSWER: Technical settings can be established for *no* reuse. This ensures that hackers who may have exploited one of the user's other business or even (and more especially) personal accounts, can less likely to be effective against corporate computer networks and assets.

ASSESSMENT OBJECTIVE *Determine if:*		
SUB-CTRL	*DESCRIPTION*	**RECOMMENDED APPROACH**
3.5.8[a]	*The number of generations during which a password cannot be reused is specified.*	NCR

3.5.8[b]	Reuse of passwords is prohibited during the specified number of generations.	NCR

ASSESSMENT METHODS AND CANDIDATE ARTIFACTS FOR REVIEW

Examine: [*SELECT FROM:* Identification and authentication policy; password policy; procedures addressing authenticator management; system security plan; system design documentation; system configuration settings and associated documentation; password configurations and associated documentation; other relevant documents or records].

Test: [*SELECT FROM:* Mechanisms supporting or implementing password-based authenticator management capability].

3.5.9 Allow temporary password use for system logons with an immediate change to a permanent password.

MINIMUM/MORE COMPLETE ANSWER: This setting is typically built into typical network operating systems. This requirement for users should be appropriately included in the recommended procedure guide.

3.5.10 Store and transmit only encrypted representation of passwords.

MINIMUM ANSWER: This is both a DIT and DAR issue, See Control 3.1.3 for a conceptual diagram. IT personnel should be regularly verifying that password data stores are always encrypted.

This control requires that all passwords are encrypted and approved by NIST's sanctioned process under FIPS 140-2. See Control 3.13.11 for the NIST website to confirm whether a cryptographic solution is approved.

MORE COMPLETE ANSWER: Suggested greater protections could require encrypted passwords are not collocated on the same main application or database server that stores significant portions of the business's data repository. A separate server (physical or virtual) could prevent hacker exploits from accessing company data stores.

ASSESSMENT OBJECTIVE *Determine if:*		
SUB-CTRL	*DESCRIPTION*	RECOMMENDED APPROACH
3.5.10[a]	*Passwords are cryptographically protected in storage.*	NCR

3.5.10[b]	Passwords are cryptographically protected in transit.	NCR

ASSESSMENT METHODS AND CANDIDATE ARTIFACTS FOR REVIEW

Examine: [*SELECT FROM:* Identification and authentication policy; password policy; procedures addressing authenticator management; system security plan; system configuration settings and associated documentation; system design documentation; password configurations and associated documentation; other relevant documents or records].

Test: [*SELECT FROM:* Mechanisms supporting or implementing password-based authenticator management capability].

3.5.11. Obscure feedback of authentication information.

MINIMUM/MORE COMPLETE ANSWER: This is like **pattern hiding** as described in Control 3.1.10. The system should prevent unauthorized individuals from compromising system-level authentication by inadvertently observing in-person ("shoulder surfing") or virtually (by viewing password entries by privileged users) remotely. It relies upon obscuring the "feedback of authentication information," for example, displaying asterisks (*) or hash symbols (#) when a user types their password. This setting should be enforced automatically and prevent general users from changing this setting.

INCIDENT RESPONSE (IR)

What do you do when you are attacked?

Incident Response (IR) primarily requires a plan, an identification of who or what agency is notified when a breach has occurred and testing of the plan over time. This control requires the development of an Incident Response Plan (IRP). There are many templates available online, and if there is an existing relationship with a State agency, companies should be able to obtain agency-specific templates.

IR is used to confirm whether an *occurrence* becomes an *event.* Based on available information about the threats within a company's IT environment, an event may or may not be raised to a defined *incident*. The IR team will determine whether the event should be raised to an actual incident for timely and actual response activities. The IR team may or may not direct what is called a **hunt**[12] to be initiated and will make that determination based on the potential or actual level of risk posed by the intrusion.

EVENT → INCIDENT

(less defined/initial occurrence) → (defined/confirmed/high impact)

Incident Response Spectrum

The first effort should be identifying with government representatives what constitutes a reportable event that formally becomes an incident. This could include a confirmed breach that has occurred to the IT infrastructure. Incidents could include anything from a Denial of Service (DOS) attack—overloading of outwardly facing web or mail servers--, or exfiltration of data—where CUI and corporate data has been copied or moved to outside of the company's firewall/perimeter. Incidents could also include the destruction of data that the company's IT staff, for example, identifies through ongoing audit activities.

Secondarily, who do you notify? The State AG Office? Do you alert your assigned Contract Officer Representative (COR), the Contract Office, DOD's US Cybercommand at Fort Meade, MD[13], or possibly the Department of Homeland Security's (DHS) Computer Emergency

---

[12] A **Hunt** is a more complex form of confirmation and action more typical of better resourced big businesses or government agencies assessing threats within their IT networks.

[13] Cybercommand will be moving to Fort Gordon, GA, in 2020.

Response Team (CERT) (https://www.us-cert.gov/forms/report)? Company representatives will have to ask their assigned COR where to file standard government "incident" reports. They should be able to provide templates and forms specific to the agency.

Finally, this security control will require testing at least ***annually***, but more often is recommended. Until comfortable with the IR "reporting chain," ***practice, practice, practice***.

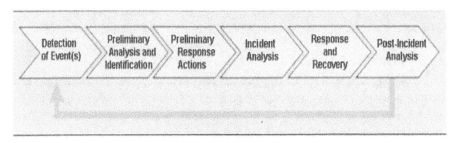

DOD Cyber Incident Life Cycle. This diagram from the DOD is a representative example of a typical "incident response life cycle." It is intended to assist in a company's approach to IR activities, and will better assist in coordination with government cybersecurity incident response organizations. Recognizing this as either an "event" (not necessarily a negative occurrence) versus an "incident" is an internal determination by the company's leadership in coordination with its security and IT professional staffs. An incident specifically requires alerting the government as soon as the intrusion is ***recognized***.

Verify with the respective agency its reporting standards. Typically, **events** may not need to be reported based on the widespread impacts and workloads to government cybersecurity response organizations. In the case of **incidents**, the standard is 72-hours; however, the recommendation is *as soon as possible* due to the potential impacts beyond the company's own IT infrastructure. It can pose a serious direct threat to State agency IT environments. Always verify this with the AG office or their designated proxy representative.

The chart below categorizes the current DOD and DHS common precedence designations. It provides both a standard categorization for identified events and typically, precedence is used to identify the level of action and response depending on the precedence "severity."

Precedence	Category	Description
0	0	Training and Exercises
1	1	Root Level Intrusion (Incident)
2	2	User Level Intrusion (Incident)
3	4	Denial of Service (Incident)
4	7	Malicious Logic (Incident)
5	3	Unsuccessful Activity Attempt (Event)
6	5	Non-Compliance Activity (Event)
7	6	Reconnaissance (Event)
8	8	Investigating (Event)
9	9	Explained Anomaly (Event)

DOD Precedence Categorization. Nine (9) is the lowest event where little is known, and IT personnel are attempting to determine whether this activity should be elevated to alert company leadership or to "close it out." One (1) is a deep attack. It identifies that the incident has gained "root" access. Root access can be construed as that the intruder has complete access to the most restrictive security levels of a system. This type of access usually is construed to complete and unfettered access to the company's network and data. (SOURCE: Cyber Incident Handling Program, CJCSM 6510.01B, 18 December 2014, http://www.jcs.mil/Portals/36/Documents/Library/Manuals/m651001.pdf?ver=2016-02-05-175710-897)

The Difference Between an 'Event' and an 'Incident'

Incident Response (IR) primarily requires a plan. It also requires the identification of who or what agency is notified when a breach has occurred.

Basic Security Requirements:

3.6.1 Establish an operational incident-handling capability for organizational information systems that includes adequate preparation, detection, analysis, containment, recovery, and user response activities.

MINIMUM ANSWER: This control addresses a "capability" that needs to be established to respond to events and incidents within the firm's IT security boundary.

This should include the **People, Process, and Technology (PPT) Model** as a recommended guide for answering many of the controls within NIST 800-171. While solutions will not necessarily require a technological answer, consideration of the people (e.g., who? what skill sets? etc.) and process (e.g., notifications to senior management, action workflows, etc.) will meet many of the response requirements.

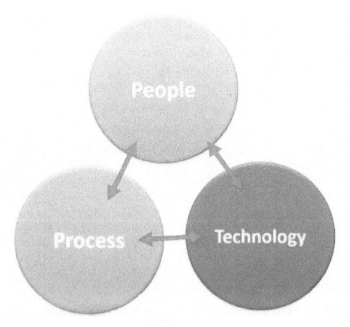

PPT Model

Use the Cyber Incident **Life Cycle** above to guide the company's operational incident-handling artifact/procedure. This should be an annex to the **SSP**. (See System Security Plan (SSP) Template and Workbook: A Supplement to "DOD NIST 800-171 Compliance Guidebook" on Amazon®). The **PPT Model** can be used to guide and formulate the IRP annex. A suggested approach using the PPT Model is described below, and includes the kinds of questions that should be answered to demonstrate best how best to formulate a good IRP:

- Preparation
  - People: Who will perform the action or activity? Training needed? Skill sets?
  - Process: Training policies for cybersecurity and IT professionals to support the IRP
  - Technology: What technology already exists to support IR? What technologies are needed?

- Detection
    - People: Are IT staff able to use audit tools properly to detect intrusions?
    - Process: What are 'best practice' approaches to detect intrusions? Monitor firewall logs? Monitor user activity?
    - Technology: Is the technology's data library current? Are automatic updates enabled?

- Analysis
    - People: Are IT staff capable of doing the analysis required? Can they determine false positive activity?
    - Process: What is the process leadership wants to get compelling and actionable data from IT staff? What are the demands for immediate and final reporting timelines?
    - Technology: Are the right tools on-site? Can open-source/web solutions useful? Can DOD or DHS provide valuable data feeds to remain current of threats?

- Containment
    - People: Can IT staff stop the ongoing attack? Do they require additional coding scripting skills to build/update firewall policies?
    - Process: Is the containment process effective? Is allowing the attack to continue to identify the threat entity/location a good idea (to support law enforcement)?
    - Technology: Can software tools quarantine and stop a malware attack? Is shutting down all external connections an excellent immediate solution (at the firewall)?

- Recovery Actions
    - People: Can the IT staff recover backup data files and media?
    - Process: What is the order of recovery? Bring up internal databases and communications first, and external servers (email and web site) be reestablished later? What are the recovery time standards for the company to regain business operations? What is acceptable? What is not acceptable?
    - Technology: Are there adequate numbers of back up devices for critical systems? Can third-party service providers assist in recovering lost or damaged data?

- User Response Activities
    - People: Can employees safely return to an operational state?

- Process: Does the company need to control access to services to select individuals first (e.g., finance, logistics, etc.)
- Technology: Can technology resolve immediate problems from the recovery vice the employee such as, for example, reselecting printers and other data connections?

MORE COMPLETE ANSWER: In those situations when control is specifically discussing a policy solution, the employment of automated tools, alerts, etc., should always be considered. Even the use of essential tracking tools such as Microsoft ® Excel ® and Access ® will at least demonstrate a level of positive control over the IT environment.

ASSESSMENT OBJECTIVE *Determine if:*		
SUB-CTRL	*DESCRIPTION*	**RECOMMENDED APPROACH**
3.6.1[a]	*An operational incident-handling capability is established.*	NCR
3.6.1[b]	*The operational incident-handling capability includes preparation.*	NCR
3.6.1[c]	*The operational incident-handling capability includes detection.*	NCR
3.6.1[d]	*The operational incident-handling capability includes analysis.*	NCR/PO/W- (It may be unreasonable for a small business to have any analytic capability other than a collection of logs and referral to the agency for action; a Waiver may be needed)
3.6.1[e]	*The operational incident-handling capability includes containment.*	NCR
3.6.1[f]	*The operational incident-handling capability includes recovery.*	NCR

3.6.1[g]	The operational incident-handling capability includes user response activities.	NCR

ASSESSMENT METHODS AND CANDIDATE ARTIFACTS FOR REVIEW

Examine: [*SELECT FROM:* Incident response policy; contingency planning policy; procedures addressing incident handling; procedures addressing incident response assistance; incident response plan; contingency plan; system security plan; procedures addressing incident response training; incident response training curriculum; incident response training materials; incident response training records; other relevant documents or records].

Test: [*SELECT FROM:* Incident-handling capability for the organization; organizational processes for incident response assistance; mechanisms supporting or implementing incident response assistance].

3.6.2 Track, document, and report incidents to appropriate officials and/or authorities both internal and external to the organization.

MINIMUM ANSWER: This control discusses the reporting requirements based on the severity of the incident as described above in DOD's Precedence Categorization diagram. Ensure some form of the repository is maintained that an auditor could review at any time. Another reminder is that such information should be secured and encrypted at least at the CUI level.

MORE COMPLETE ANSWER: A complete response may include a dedicated computer server repository that could be physically disconnected from the system when not needed. This could prevent unauthorized access if an intruder is attempting to conduct intelligence collection or **reconnaissance** of the system; this would deny intruders critical network information and add confusion for their penetration activities.

ASSESSMENT OBJECTIVE *Determine if:*		
SUB-CTRL	*DESCRIPTION*	**RECOMMENDED APPROACH**
3.6.2[a]	Incidents are tracked.	NCR
3.6.2[b]	Incidents are documented.	NCR
3.6.2[c]	Authorities to whom incidents are to be reported are identified.	NCR
3.6.2[d]	Organizational officials to whom incidents are to be reported are identified.	NCR
3.6.2[e]	Identified authorities are notified of incidents.	NCR

3.6.2[f]	*Identified organizational officials are notified of incidents.*	NCR

ASSESSMENT METHODS AND CANDIDATE ARTIFACTS FOR REVIEW

Examine: [*SELECT FROM:* Incident response policy; procedures addressing incident monitoring; incident response records and documentation; procedures addressing incident reporting; incident reporting records and documentation; incident response plan; system security plan; other relevant documents or records].

Test: [*SELECT FROM:* Incident monitoring capability for the organization; mechanisms supporting or implementing tracking and documenting of system security incidents; organizational processes for incident reporting; mechanisms supporting or implementing incident reporting].

Derived Security Requirements:

3.6.3 Test the organizational incident response capability.

MINIMUM ANSWER: Test the IR Plan at least annually. This should include both internal and external notional penetration exercises. These may include compromised login information and passwords provided to designated IT personnel. Ensure the results of the test are documented, reviewed, and signed by senior management. An IR test event should be maintained for any future audit.

MORE COMPLETE ANSWER: This is not a requirement of this control and poses many risks to the IT environment. Do not recommend this solution; this would only be required based on the sensitivity of data, and Penetration Testing (PENTEST) is directed by the government. It is only offered for more of an appreciation of the complexity that a PENTEST entails.

A more expensive solution is hiring an outside Penetration Testing (PENTEST) company. Ensure that Rules of Engagement (ROE) are well established. Rules that should be affirmed by both the company and the PENTESTER, for example, is that no inadvertent change or destruction of data is authorized. The PENTEST company may also require a liability release for any unintentional damage caused by the PENTEST. Always coordinate with legal professionals experienced in such matters to avoid any damage or confusion created by unclear expectations of a PENTEST.

MAINTENANCE (MA)

How do you take care of IT?

The MA security control is relatively easy to address with regards to the requirements of NIST 800-171. This control requires processes and procedures that provide oversight of third-party vendors that offer IT maintenance and support. While this may appear vaguely paranoid, the company is required to exercise control of all maintenance personnel that potentially will have access to the company's and government's resident CUI and data. This will also typically require company escorts whose background have been appropriately checked and authorized to oversee outside workers.

Lack of maintenance or a failure to perform maintenance can result in the unauthorized disclosure of CUI. The full implementation of this requirement is contingent on the finalization of the proposed CUI State regulation and marking guidance in the **CUI Registry**. (The marking requirements have been completed, and it is best to refer to the Registry, https://www.archives.gov/cui/registry/category-list, for specified industry codes.) These markings should be applied to business CUI data as well as IT hardware such as servers, desktops, laptops, etc.

Basic Security Requirements:

3.7.1 Perform maintenance on organizational information systems.

MINIMUM ANSWER: This should describe the company's maintenance procedures for its IT infrastructure. This could include either internal maintenance teams or third-party companies. This will include hardware component repairs and replacements, printer repairs, etc. Any maintenance agreements should be provided as artifacts to support an authorization package.

MORE COMPLETE ANSWER: Maintenance could include the identification of computer hardware spares on-site or at company warehouse locations. Operational spares should be managed by the company's logistics' personnel; they should be captured within the property book database and its associated hard copy reporting to senior management.

3.7.2 Provide effective controls on the tools, techniques, mechanisms, and personnel used to conduct information system maintenance.

MINIMUM ANSWER: This control relates to tools used for diagnostics and repairs of the company's IT system/network. These tools include, for example, hardware/software diagnostic test equipment and hardware/software **packet sniffers**. Access to the hardware tools should be secured in lockable containers, and only accessed by authorized IT personnel.

In the case of software tools, they should be restricted to personnel with privileged user rights and individually audited when any use is required or needed.

MORE COMPLETE ANSWER: Suggested additional control may include two-person integrity requirements. This would require that when any of these types of tools are utilized, there should be at least two authorized individuals involved in any system maintenance or diagnostic activities.

ASSESSMENT OBJECTIVE *Determine if:*		
SUB-CTRL	*DESCRIPTION*	**RECOMMENDED APPROACH**
3.7.2[a]	*Tools used to conduct system maintenance are controlled.*	NCR
3.7.2[b]	*Techniques used to conduct system maintenance are controlled.*	NCR
3.7.2[c]	*Mechanisms used to conduct system maintenance are controlled.*	NCR
3.7.2[d]	*Personnel used to conduct system maintenance are controlled.*	NCR

ASSESSMENT METHODS AND CANDIDATE ARTIFACTS FOR REVIEW

Examine: [*SELECT FROM:* System maintenance policy; procedures addressing system-maintenance tools and media; maintenance records; system-maintenance tools and associated documentation; maintenance tool inspection records; system security plan; other relevant documents or records].

Test: [*SELECT FROM:* Organizational processes for approving, controlling, and monitoring maintenance tools; mechanisms supporting or implementing approval, control, and monitoring of maintenance tools; organizational processes for inspecting maintenance tools; mechanisms supporting or implementing inspection of maintenance tools; organizational process for inspecting media for malicious code; mechanisms supporting or implementing inspection of media used for maintenance].

Derived Security Requirements:

3.7.3 Ensure equipment removed for off-site maintenance is sanitized of any CUI.

MINIMUM ANSWER: Company data should be backed-up locally and secured for a future reinstall on another storage device or the returned/repaired IT component. Also, the data should specifically be "wiped" by an industry-standard application for data deletion. There are many software tools that conduct multiple "passes" of data wipes to ensure sanitization of the media.

MORE COMPLETE ANSWER: Any reports produced by the data "wiping" program could be captured in an equipment data log to provide proof of the action. Maintaining a hard copy of a soft copy spreadsheet or database log would be helpful. Future inspections by the government may check this procedure to confirm the continuous application and repeatability of this procedure.

3.7.4 Check media containing diagnostic and test programs for malicious code before the media are used in the information system.

MINIMUM ANSWER: The ideal solution for this is to conduct a scan using corporate anti-virus software applications.

MORE COMPLETE ANSWER: A more thorough solution would include the use of an anti-malware application. Anti-malware programs are more comprehensive and proactively monitor **endpoints**, i.e., computers, laptops, servers, etc. (Anti-virus is not always designed to identify and clean malware, adware, worms, etc., from infected storage devices).

3.7.5 Require multifactor authentication to establish nonlocal maintenance sessions via external network connections and terminate such connections when nonlocal maintenance is complete.

MINIMUM ANSWER: Nonlocal maintenance is those diagnostic or repair activities conducted over network communications to include the Internet or dedicated least circuits.

This requires that any external third-party maintenance activities use some form of Multi-Factor Authentication (MFA) to directly access company IT hardware and software components. If IT personnel, working with outside maintainers can use an MFA solution, then the company most likely has a robust IT support capability. If not, then this control is a right candidate for an early POAM; ensure good milestones are established for monthly review, for example, "on-going research," "market survey of potential candidate solutions," "identification of funding sources," etc.

MORE COMPLETE ANSWER: A complete answer requires a technical solution. As discussed earlier, the use of CAC, PIV cards, or tokens, such as the RSA ® rotating encryption keying devices are ideal solutions. This solution most likely will require additional analysis and funding approaches to select the most appropriate answer.

ASSESSMENT OBJECTIVE *Determine if:*		
SUB-CTRL	*DESCRIPTION*	**RECOMMENDED APPROACH**
3.7.5[a]	*Multifactor authentication is used to establish nonlocal maintenance sessions via external network connections.*	NCR
3.7.5[b]	*Nonlocal maintenance sessions established via external network connections are terminated when nonlocal maintenance is complete.*	NCR
ASSESSMENT METHODS AND CANDIDATE ARTIFACTS FOR REVIEW		

Examine: [*SELECT FROM:* System maintenance policy; procedures addressing nonlocal system maintenance; system security plan; system design documentation; system configuration settings and associated documentation; maintenance records; diagnostic records; other relevant documents or records].

Test: [*SELECT FROM:* Organizational processes for managing nonlocal maintenance; mechanisms implementing, supporting, and managing nonlocal maintenance; mechanisms for strong authentication of nonlocal maintenance diagnostic sessions; mechanisms for terminating nonlocal maintenance sessions and network connections].

3.7.6 Supervise the maintenance activities of maintenance personnel without required access authorization.

MINIMUM ANSWER: The procedure requirement should reflect that non-company maintenance personnel should always be escorted. An access log should be maintained, and it should include, for example, the individual or individuals, the represented company, the equipment repaired/diagnosed, the arrival and departure times, and the assigned escort.

Maintain this hard-copy of soft-copy logs for future auditing purposes.

MORE COMPLETE ANSWER: Procedural enhancements could include confirmed background checks of third-party maintainers and picture identification compared with the on-site individual. These additional enhancements should be based upon the sensitivity of the company's data. Any unattended CUI data should always be secured by CUI procedures—in a lockable container.

MEDIA PROTECTION (MP)
Create, protect, and destroy

The MP control was written to handle the challenges of managing and protecting the computer media storing CUI. This would include the governments' concerns about removable hard drives and especially the ability for a threat employ the use of a Universal Serial Bus (USB) "thumb drive."

While most computer users are aware of the convenience of the thumb drive to help store, transfer, and maintain data, it is also a well-known threat vector where criminals and foreign threats can introduce dangerous malware and viruses into unsuspecting users' computers; the DOD forbids their use except under particular and controlled instances.

MP is also about assurances by the business that proper destruction and sanitization of old storage devices has occurred. There are many instances where State agencies have not implemented an effective sanitization process, and inadvertent disclosure of national security data has been released to the public. Cases include salvage companies discovering hard drives and disposed of computers containing CUI and, in several cases, national security classified information, has occurred.

Be especially mindful that the sanitization process requires high-grade industry or government-approved applications that entirely and effectively destroys all data on the target drive. Other processes may include physical shredding of the drive or destruction methods that further prevent the reconstruction of any virtual data by unauthorized personnel.

Basic Security Requirements:

3.8.1 Protect (i.e., physically control and securely store) information system media containing CUI, both paper and digital.

MINIMUM ANSWER: To implement this control, the business should establish procedures regarding both CUI physical and virtual (disk drives) media. This should include only authorized personnel having access to individual and corporate sensitive data with necessary background checks and training. A business can use the foundations of other control families to mitigate further or reduce risks/threats.

A company can use other controls such as *more* training, longer audit log retention, *more* guards, or *more* complex passwords to **mitigate** any control. This would more clearly demonstrate to the government that the firm has an actual implementation of these security controls.

The use of other mitigating controls within NIST 800-171 are specifically about **risk reduction.** Any effort to use other families of controls to meet a specific control improves the overall IT infrastructure's security posture and is highly recommended.

MORE COMPLETE ANSWER: The MP control can be further demonstrated by safeguarding physical files in secure or fire-resistant vaults. This could also include requirements for only IT personnel issuing property hand receipts for computer equipment or devices; a sound accountability system is essential.

ASSESSMENT OBJECTIVE *Determine if:*		
SUB-CTRL	*DESCRIPTION*	**RECOMMENDED APPROACH**
3.8.1[a]	*Paper media containing CUI is physically controlled.*	NCR
3.8.1[b]	*Digital media containing CUI is physically controlled.*	NCR
3.8.1[c]	*Paper media containing CUI is securely stored.*	NCR (Typically demonstrated by securing within a lockable container, desk, etc., and the individual/s authorized access are the only one's identified to enter, remove, or destroy CUI data from its holding area.)
3.8.1[d]	*Digital media containing CUI is securely stored.*	NCR

3.8.2 Limit access to CUI on information system media to authorized users.

MINIMUM ANSWER: Identify in policy documents which, by name, title, or function, has access to specified CUI. Any artifacts should include the policy document and an associated by-name roster of personnel assigned access by-system, e.g., accounting system, ordering system, patent repository, medical records, etc.

MORE COMPLETE ANSWER: A complete response could include logging of authorized personnel and providing a print-out of accesses over one month.

3.8.3 Sanitize or destroy information system media containing CUI before disposal or release for reuse.

MINIMUM ANSWER: A good policy description is a must regarding data destruction of sensitive information within the government. Either use a commercial-grade "wiping" program or physically destroy the drive.

If the company is either planning to internally reuse or sell to outside repurposing companies, ensure that the wiping is commercial grade or approved by the government. There are companies providing disk shredding or destruction services. Provide any service agreements that should specify the type and level of data destruction to government assessors.

MORE COMPLETE ANSWER: For any assessment, the media sanitization company should provide **destruction certificates**. Chose several selected destruction certificates to include in the BOE submission. Typically, logistics and supply ordering sections of the business should manage as part of the Supply Chain Risk Management (SCRM) process.

ASSESSMENT OBJECTIVE *Determine if:*		
SUB-CTRL	*DESCRIPTION*	**RECOMMENDED APPROACH**
3.8.3[a]	*System media containing CUI is sanitized or destroyed before disposal.*	NCR
3.8.3[b]	*System media containing CUI is sanitized before it is released for reuse.*	NCR

ASSESSMENT METHODS AND CANDIDATE ARTIFACTS FOR REVIEW

Examine: [*SELECT FROM:* System media protection policy; procedures addressing media sanitization and disposal; applicable standards and policies addressing media sanitization; system security plan; media sanitization records; system audit logs and records; system design documentation; system configuration settings and associated documentation; other relevant documents or records].

Test: [*SELECT FROM:* Organizational processes for media sanitization; mechanisms supporting or implementing media sanitization].

A QUICK DISCUSSION ON SUPPLY CHAIN RISK MANAGEMENT

SCRM is a relatively new concern within State and Federal governments. It is part of securing IT products within the business.

Questions that should be considered include:

- Is this product produced by the US or by an Ally?
- Could counterfeit IT items be purchased from less-than-reputable entities?
- Is this IT product from an approved hardware/software product listing?

Users innately trust software developers to provide security updates for their software applications and products that would add new functionalities or fix security vulnerabilities. They would not expect updates to be infected with malicious scripts, codes, or programming. Most users have no mechanisms (or no concerns) about defending against seemingly legitimate software that is duly signed. Unfortunately, software unwittingly accessed by users and tainted by either nation-state actors or general cyber-criminals on the Internet poses an alarming risk to the global IT supply chain.

The use of separate supply chain attacks by cyber attackers to access corporate software development infrastructures has been major vectors of concerns for the government as well as the private sector. These attacks typically include targeting publicly connected software build, test, update servers, and other portions of a software company's software development environment. Nation-state agents can then inject malware into software updates and releases have far-ranging impacts on the IT supply chain; the challenge continues to grow.[14]

Users become infected through official software distribution channels that are trusted. Attackers can add their malware to the development infrastructure of software vendors before they are compiled[15]; hence, the malware is signed with the digital identity of a legitimate software vendor. This exploit bypasses typical "whitelisting" security measures making it difficult to identify the intrusion. This has contributed to a high degree of success by malicious cyber threat actors. Some example recent intrusions include:

- In July 2017, Chinese cyber espionage operatives changed the software packages of a legitimate software vendor, NetSarang Computer (https://www.netsarang.com/). These changes allowed access to a broad range of industries and institutions that included retail locations, financial services, transportation, telecommunications, energy, media, and academic.

- In August 2017, hackers inserted a backdoor into updates of the computer "cleanup" program, **CCleaner** while it was in its software development phases.

- In June 2017, suspected Russian actors **deployed the** PETYA ransomware to a wide-range of European targets by compromising a targeted Ukrainian software vendor

Another recent example of a supply chain compromise occurred in 2017. During this incident, Dell **lost** control of a customer support website and its associated Internet web address. Control of the website was wrested from a Dell support contractor that had failed to renew its authorized domain license and fees. The site was designed specifically to assist customers in the restoration of their computer and its data when infected. There were following signs that the domain may have been infecting customers; two weeks after the contractor lost control of the address, the server that hosted the domain began appearing in numerous malware alerts.

---

[14] Other less-protected portions of the supply chain include, for example, Field Programmable Gate Arrays (FPGA) and Application-Specific Integrated Circuit (ASIC) chips found on most major US weapons and satellite systems.
[15] Before they are converted as an executable (.exe) that are injected at the programming level where quality control mechanisms are often less-than adequate in secure development processes

The site was purchased by **TeamInternet.com,** a German company that specializes in Uniform Resource Locator (URL) hijacking and typosquatting[16] type exploits. (This company could also sell or lease the domain to anyone at that point to include back to Dell). They took advantage of users believing they were going to a legitimate site and then being redirected to this redesigned malware site.

Supply chain compromises have been seen for years, but they have been mostly isolated and covert[17]. They may follow with subsequent intrusions into targets of interest much later and provide a means for general hacking and damage to the company targets. The use of such a compromise provides highly likely means to support nation-state cyber-espionage activities, including those identified from Chinese IT equipment product builders. These include such companies such as Chinese-based companies to include ZTE, Lenovo, and Huawei.

This trend continues to grow as there are more points in the supply chain that the attackers can penetrate using advanced techniques. The techniques involved have become publicly discussed enough, and their proven usefulness encourages others to use these vectors of attack specific to damage and reconnaissance of governments, businesses, and agencies globally. Advanced actors will likely continue to leverage this activity to conduct cyber espionage, cybercrime, and disruption. The dangers to the supply chain are of growing concern as the threat and risk landscapes continue to increase for the foreseeable future.

For further information, see NIST 800-161, *Supply Chain Risk Management Practices for Federal Information Systems and Organizations.*
(http://nvlpubs.nist.gov/nistpubs/SpecialPublications/NIST.SP.800-161.pdf).

Derived Security Requirements:

3.8.4 Mark media with necessary CUI markings and distribution limitations.
MINIMUM ANSWER: This includes the marking of both physical documents as well as soft-copy versions. The best way to answer this is by referencing the following National Archives and Record Administration (NARA) document as part of the company's procedural guide that addresses this control:

---

[16] **Typosquatting** is a form of Uniform Resource Locator (URL) hijacking and can be described as a form of cybersquatting and possibly brandjacking (e.g., Pepsie.com). It relies on mistakes by the individual especially due to "typos." It causes redirects using subtle and common variations in spellings to both malicious and marketing (adware) sites.
[17] Disclosing such information by a business may have both legal and reputation impacts; current US law under the 2015 Computer Information Security Act (CISA) does allow for "safe harbor" protections in the US.

- *Marking Controlled Unclassified Information*, Version 1.1 – December 6, 2016. (https://www.archives.gov/files/cui/20161206-cui-marking-handbook-v1-1.pdf)

EXAMPLE PROCEDURE: All company personnel will mark CUI, physical and virtual data, following the National Archives and Record Administration (NARA), Marking Controlled Unclassified Information, Version 1.1 – December 6, 2016. If there are questions about marking requirements, employees will refer these questions to their immediate supervisor or the corporate CUI officer."

MORE COMPLETE ANSWER: This could include a screen capture that shows a government representative that onscreen access to CUI data is appropriately marked. A firm could also assign a CUI marking specialist; this person should be an individual with prior security experience and familiar with marking requirements. For example, this individual could additionally provide quarterly "brown bag" sessions where the "CUI Security Officer" provides training during lunchtime sessions. Be creative when considering more thorough means to reinforce cybersecurity control requirements.

ASSESSMENT OBJECTIVE *Determine if:*		
SUB-CTRL	*DESCRIPTION*	**RECOMMENDED APPROACH**
3.8.4[a]	*Media containing CUI is marked with applicable CUI markings.*	NCR
3.8.4[b]	*Media containing CUI is marked with distribution limitations.*	NCR
ASSESSMENT METHODS AND CANDIDATE ARTIFACTS FOR REVIEW		
<u>Examine</u>: [*SELECT FROM:* System media protection policy; procedures addressing media marking; physical and environmental protection policy and procedures; system security plan; list of system media marking security attributes; designated controlled areas; other relevant documents or records].		
<u>Test</u>: [*SELECT FROM:* Organizational processes for marking information media; mechanisms supporting or implementing media marking].		

3.8.5 Control access to media containing CUI and maintain accountability for media during transport outside of controlled areas.

MINIMUM ANSWER: This control is about "transport outside of controlled areas." This too is a matter of only authorized individuals (couriers) be authorized by position, training, and security checks that should be considered when the company needs to transport CUI external to its typical corporate location.

Individuals should be provided either courier cards or orders that are signed by an authorized company representative typically responsible for oversight of security matters. This could be, for example, the corporate security officer, Information System Security Manager (ISSM), or their designated representative. These individuals should be readily known to other employees and managers who have demanded to move CUI to outside locations. This would demonstrate that there are available and on-call personnel based on the business mission and priorities. This also should be a limited cadre of personnel that management relies on for such external courier services.

MORE COMPLETE ANSWER: The company could hire an outside contract service that transports both physical and computer media containing CUI based on the company's mission.

ASSESSMENT OBJECTIVE *Determine if:*		
SUB-CTRL	*DESCRIPTION*	**RECOMMENDED APPROACH**
3.8.5[a]	*Access to media containing CUI is controlled.*	NCR
3.8.5[b]	*Accountability for media containing CUI is maintained during transport outside of controlled areas.*	NCR

ASSESSMENT METHODS AND CANDIDATE ARTIFACTS FOR REVIEW

Examine: [*SELECT FROM:* System media protection policy; procedures are addressing media storage; physical and environmental protection policy and procedures; access control policy and procedures; system security plan; system media; designated controlled areas; other relevant documents or records].

Test: [*SELECT FROM:* Organizational processes for storing media; mechanisms supporting or implementing media storage and media protection].

3.8.6 Implement cryptographic mechanisms to protect the confidentiality of CUI stored on digital media during transport unless otherwise protected by alternative physical safeguards.

MINIMUM ANSWER: This is a Data at Rest (DAR) issue. See Control 3.1.3 for depiction. The recommendation is that all CUI needs to be encrypted. A typical application that has been used is BitLocker ®. It provides password protection to "lockdown" any transportable media. It is not the only solution, and there are many solutions that can be used to secure DAR.

The 256-bit key length is the universal standard for commercial and government encryption applications for hard drives, removable drives, and even USB devices. The government requires DAR must always be encrypted; it is best to resource and research acceptable tools that the government supports and recognizes.

MORE COMPLETE ANSWER: The reinforcing of this control may include using enhanced physical security measures. This could include hardened and lockable carry cases. Only authorized employees should transport designated CUI. This should also be captured in the submitted BOE.

3.8.7 Control the use of removable media on information system components.

MINIMUM ANSWER: Identify in corporate policy the types and kinds of removable media that can be attached to fixed desktop and laptop computers. These could include external hard drives, optical drives, or USB thumb drives.

Strongly recommend that thumb drives are not used; if needed, then designate IT security personnel who can authorize their restricted use. This should also include anti-virus/malware scans before their use.

MORE COMPLETE ANSWER: Removeable media drives can be "blocked" by changes in system **registry** settings; company IT personnel should be able to prevent such designated devices from accessing the computer and accessing the company network.

3.8.8 Prohibit the use of portable storage devices when such devices have no identifiable owner.

MINIMUM ANSWER: This should be established in the company procedure. If such devices are found, they should be surrendered to security and scanned immediately for any viruses, malware, etc.

MORE COMPLETE ANSWER: As described in Control 3.8.7, IT personnel can block unauthorized devices from attaching to the computer/network by updating registry settings.

3.8.9 Protect the confidentiality of backup CUI at storage locations.

MINIMUM ANSWER: *This is a Data at Rest (DAR) issue.* See Control 3.1.3 for a depiction. See Control 3.8.6 for suggested requirements for the protection of CUI under a DAR solution.

MORE COMPLETE ANSWER: See Control 3.8.6 for additional means to protect CUI.

PERSONNEL SECURITY (PS)
Background Checks

This is a relatively simple control. It most likely is already implemented within the company and only requires procedural documents are provided in the submission. This should include both civil and criminal background checks using a reputable company that can process the individual background checks through the Federal Bureau of Investigation (FBI). Background Checking companies can also do other forms of personnel checks to include individual social media presence or financial solvency matters that may avoid any future embarrassment for the company.

While these checks are not well defined for the company's under NIST 800-171, it should meet minimum government standards for a **Public Trust** review. Discuss with the AG Office or their designated proxy representative the requirements they suggest being met to provide the level of background check required to meet the NIST 800-171 requirement. Also, it is always best to work with HR and legal experts when formulating a personnel security policy to include the types and kinds of investigations are per applicable state and federal law in this area.

Basic Security Requirements:

3.9.1 Screen individuals prior to authorizing access to information systems containing CUI.

MINIMUM ANSWER: This control requires some form of background check to be conducted for employees. There are several firms that can provide criminal and civil background checks based upon an individual's personal information and their fingerprints.

The company should capture its HR process regarding background checks in the company cybersecurity procedure document. It is also essential to address when a reinvestigation is required. The suggestion is at least every three years or upon recognition by managers of potential legal occurrences that may include financial problems, domestic violence, etc. This control should be highly integrated with the company HR and legal policies.

MORE COMPLETE ANSWER: Some background companies can, for an additional fee, conduct active monitoring of individuals when significant personal or financial changes occur in a person's life — update company procedural guides with all details of the company's established process.

3.9.2 Ensure that CUI and information systems containing CUI are protected during and after personnel actions such as terminations and transfers.

MINIMUM ANSWER: This control is about procedures regarding whether termination is amicable or not. Always have clear terms about non-removal of corporate data and CUI after departure from the company to include databases, customer listings, and proprietary data/IP. This should include legal implications for violation of the policy.

MORE COMPLETE ANSWER: The technical solution could include monitoring by IT staff of all account activity during the out-processing period. This could also include immediate account lock-outs on the departure date. Also recommend that there are changes to all vault combinations, building accesses, etc., that the individual had specific access to during their tenure.

ASSESSMENT OBJECTIVE *Determine if:*		
SUB-CTRL	*DESCRIPTION*	**RECOMMENDED APPROACH**
3.9.2[a]	*A policy and/or process for terminating system access and any credentials coincident with personnel actions is established.*	NCR
3.9.2[b]	*System access and credentials are terminated consistent with personnel actions such as termination or transfer.*	NCR
3.9.2[c]	*The system is protected during and after personnel transfer actions.*	P- An update should include changes or updates in accesses when an employee transfers to another location or office.

Derived Security Requirements: None.

PHYSICAL PROTECTION (PP)
Guards and moats....

Physical security is part of a company's overall protection of its people and facilities. A little-known fact is that the guiding principle for any *true* cybersecurity professional is to protect the life and safety of the people supported. This control is also about the protection of damage to corporate assets, facilities, or equipment; this includes any loss or destruction of the material computer equipment secured by the PP security control. This controls addresses the physical security that also includes such elements as guards, alarm systems, cameras, etc., that help the company protect its sensitive company data and, of course, its NIST 800-171 CUI.

There are no limits on how to harden a company's "castle walls," but for any owner, the cost is always a significant consideration. Protecting vital CUI while seemingly expansive under this control allows for cognitive flexibility. Again, the company should reasonably define its success under the NIST 800-171 controls. "Success" can be defined from the company's point of view regarding complexity or cost but must be prepared to defend any proposed solution to government assessors.

Basic Security Requirements:

3.10.1 Limit physical access to organizational information systems, equipment, and the respective operating environments to authorized individuals.
MINIMUM ANSWER: Of importance for this control, is limiting access to corporate data servers, backup devices, and specifically, the "computer farm." If the company is maintaining devices on its premises, then policy should address who has authorized access to such sensitive areas.

If the corporation is using an off-site **Cloud Service Provider (CSP)**, capture in part or full sections of any CSP service agreements specific to physical security measures, both types of computer architectures should address for example areas of interest such as access logs, after-hours access, camera monitoring, unauthorized access reporting criteria, types, and kinds of network defense devices such as Intrusion Detection and Prevention Systems (IDS/IPS), etc., as part of the corporate procedure.

MORE COMPLETE ANSWER: This could include active alerting to both management and security personnel that includes phone calls, email alerts, or SMS text messages to designated company security personnel. Security measures and **alert thresholds** should be driven by the sensitivity of the data stored. Management should make **risk-based** determinations of the cost and returns on effectiveness to drive the corporate policy for this control as well as other solutions.

ASSESSMENT OBJECTIVE *Determine if:*		
SUB-CTRL	*DESCRIPTION*	**RECOMMENDED APPROACH**
3.10.1[a]	*Authorized individuals allowed physical access are identified.*	NCR
3.10.1[b]	*Physical access to organizational systems is limited to authorized individuals.*	NCR
3.10.1[c]	*Physical access to equipment is limited to authorized individuals.*	NCR
3.10.1[d]	*Physical access to operating environments is limited to authorized individuals.*	NCR

ASSESSMENT METHODS AND CANDIDATE ARTIFACTS FOR REVIEW

Examine: [*SELECT FROM:* Physical and environmental protection policy; procedures addressing physical access authorizations; system security plan; authorized personnel access list; authorization credentials; physical access list reviews; physical access termination records and associated documentation; other relevant documents or records].

Test: [*SELECT FROM:* Organizational processes for physical access authorizations; mechanisms supporting or implementing physical access authorizations].

3.10.2 Protect and monitor the physical facility and support infrastructure for those information systems.

MINIMUM/MORE COMPLETE ANSWER: This control can be addressed in many ways by physical security measures. This should include locked doors, cipher locks, safes, security cameras, guard forces, etc. This control should be answered by the current physical protections that prevent direct entry into the company and physical access to its IT devices and networks.

ASSESSMENT OBJECTIVE *Determine if:*		
SUB-CTRL	*DESCRIPTION*	**RECOMMENDED APPROACH**
3.10.2[a]	*The physical facility where organizational systems reside is protected.*	NCR
3.10.2[b]	*The support infrastructure for organizational systems is protected.*	NCR- (This would include all physical barriers to entries into computer spaces, server rooms, etc., for unauthorized personnel)
3.10.2[c]	*The physical facility where organizational systems reside is monitored.*	NCR - (typically, cameras or guards)
3.10.2[d]	*The support infrastructure for organizational systems is monitored.*	NCR

ASSESSMENT METHODS AND CANDIDATE ARTIFACTS FOR REVIEW

Examine: [*SELECT FROM:* Physical and environmental protection policy; procedures addressing physical access monitoring; system security plan; physical access logs or records; physical access monitoring records; physical access log reviews; other relevant documents or records].

Test: [*SELECT FROM:* Organizational processes for monitoring physical access; mechanisms supporting or implementing physical access monitoring; mechanisms supporting or implementing the review of physical access logs].

Derived Security Requirements:

3.10.3 Escort visitors and monitor visitor activity.

MINIMUM ANSWER: Much as described under the MA control above, like security measures as described in Control 3.7.6 should be employed.

MORE COMPLETE ANSWER: Also, refer to Control 3.7.6 on more significant security measures that can be used to demonstrate complete compliance with this control.

ASSESSMENT OBJECTIVE *Determine if:*		
SUB-CTRL	*DESCRIPTION*	**RECOMMENDED APPROACH**
3.10.3[a]	*Visitors are escorted.*	NCR

3.10.3[b]	*Visitor activity is monitored.*	NCR – (Escorts, guards, and cameras inclusive)

ASSESSMENT METHODS AND CANDIDATE ARTIFACTS FOR REVIEW

Examine: [*SELECT FROM:* Physical and environmental protection policy; procedures addressing physical access control; system security plan; physical access control logs or records; inventory records of physical access control devices; system entry and exit points; records of key and lock combination changes; storage locations for physical access control devices; physical access control devices; list of security safeguards controlling access to designated publicly accessible areas within facility; other relevant documents or records].

Test: [*SELECT FROM:* Organizational processes for physical access control; mechanisms supporting or implementing physical access control; physical access control devices].

3.10.4 Maintain audit logs of physical access.

MINIMUM/MORE COMPLETE ANSWER: Refer to Control 3.7.6 for suggested audit log items. This should address personnel during operating and after-hour entry into the company and its IT facilities. This should include logs specific to outside third-party vendors and subcontractors; any such procedures should also apply to those individuals who are not direct employees.

3.10.5 Control and manage physical access devices.

MINIMUM ANSWER: This control requires that physical access devices such as security badges, combinations, and physical keys are managed through both procedure and logs (physical or automated). The company needs to demonstrate to the government its positive security measures to protect its CUI data. While this control may appear more comfortable than the technical policy control settings used by the company for its IT systems, it is no less critical.

MORE COMPLETE ANSWER: If not already in place, identify and separate the physical security functions (e.g., facility security officer, etc.) from the technical security functions managed by corporate IT personnel with the requisite skills and experiences. Companies should avoid duty-creep on its cybersecurity personnel and define roles and responsibilities between its classic security functions (e.g., physical, personnel security, etc.) and the roles and responsibilities of its cyber workforce that may reduce their effectiveness of both security areas.

ASSESSMENT OBJECTIVE *Determine if:*		
SUB-CTRL	*DESCRIPTION*	RECOMMENDED APPROACH
3.10.5[a]	*Physical access devices are identified.*	NCR
3.10.5[b]	*Physical access devices are controlled.*	NCR
3.10.5[c]	*Physical access devices are managed.*	NCR

ASSESSMENT METHODS AND CANDIDATE ARTIFACTS FOR REVIEW

Examine: [*SELECT FROM:* Physical and environmental protection policy; procedures addressing physical access control; system security plan; physical access control logs or records; inventory records of physical access control devices; system entry and exit points; records of key and lock combination changes; storage locations for physical access control devices; physical access control devices; list of security safeguards controlling access to designated publicly accessible areas within facility; other relevant documents or records].

Test: [*SELECT FROM:* Organizational processes for physical access control; mechanisms supporting or implementing physical access control; physical access control devices].

Cybersecurity workforce duty-creep is a real-world occurrence; Companies are unwittingly shifting overall "security" functions from classic security personnel to cybersecurity professionals creating security gaps for a company or agency

---

3.10.6 Enforce safeguarding measures for CUI at alternate work sites (e.g., telework sites).

MINIMUM ANSWER: (See Control 3.1.3 for the explanation of DAR and DIT). This control can be quickly addressed by DAR application solutions. Laptops should always be password protected; this should be part of any central cybersecurity policy document and enforced by technical solutions deployed by company IT personnel. Additionally, The DIT protections are afforded by corporate VPN and 2FA/MFA solutions.

MORE COMPLETE ANSWER: The company should establish minimum requirements for telework protection. This could include, for example, work should be conducted in a physically securable area, the VPN should always be used, corporate assets should not use unsecured networks such as at coffee shops, fast-food restaurants, etc. This could also include an explicit telework agreement for employees before being authorized telework permission, and it should be carefully coordinated with HR and legal experts.

ASSESSMENT OBJECTIVE *Determine if:*		
SUB-CTRL	*DESCRIPTION*	**RECOMMENDED APPROACH**
3.10.6[a]	*Safeguarding measures for CUI are defined for alternate work sites.*	NCR
3.10.6[b]	*Safeguarding measures for CUI are enforced for alternate work sites.*	NCR

ASSESSMENT METHODS AND CANDIDATE ARTIFACTS FOR REVIEW

Examine: [*SELECT FROM:* Physical and environmental protection policy; procedures addressing alternate work sites for personnel; system security plan; list of safeguards required for alternate work sites; assessments of safeguards at alternate work sites; other relevant documents or records].

Test: [*SELECT FROM:* Organizational processes for security at alternate work sites; mechanisms supporting alternate work sites; safeguards employed at alternate work sites; means of communications between personnel at alternate work sites and security personnel].

RISK ASSESSMENT (RA)
Dealing with Changes to the Infrastructure

The RA control relies on a continual process to determine whether changes in hardware, software or architecture create either a significant positive or negative **security-relevant** effect. This is typically done by using a **Change Request** (CR). If an upgrade to, for example, the Window 10 ® Secure Host Baseline Operating System software, and it improves the security posture of the network, a Risk Assessment (RA) is needed and associated **risk analysis** should be performed by authorized technical personnel. This could take the form of a technical report that management accepts from its IT staff for approval or disapproval of the change. Management, working with its IT staff, should determine thresholds when a formal RA activity needs to occur.

The RA process affords a considerable amount of flexibility during the life of the system and should be used when other-than, for example, a new application or **security patches** are applied. Security patches updates are typically integrated into Operating Systems and applications. IT personnel should also regularly manually check for regular functional patches and security patch updates from the software companies' websites.

"Negative" security-relevant effects on the corporate IT infrastructure include, for example, a major re-architecture event or a move to a Cloud Service Provider. While these events may not seem "negative," NIST standards require a full reassessment. In other words, plan accordingly if the company is going to embark on a significant overhaul of its IT system. There will be a need under these circumstances to consider the impacts on the company's current Authority to Operate (ATO). These types of event typically necessitate that the NIST 800-171 process is redone; prior work in terms of policies and procedures can be reused to receive an updated ATO.

The decision-tree below is designed to help a company determine when to consider an RA:

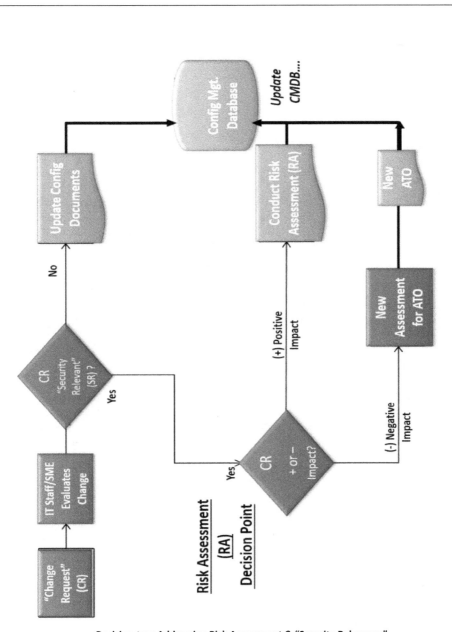

Decision-tree Addressing Risk Assessment & "Security Relevance"

Basic Security Requirements:

3.11.1 Periodically assess the risk to organizational operations (including mission, functions, image, or reputation), organizational assets, and individuals, resulting from the operation of organizational information systems and the associated processing, storage, or transmission of CUI.

MINIMUM ANSWER: RA's are required when there is a "major" change due to either a hardware change (e.g., replacing an old firewall with a new Cisco ® firewall), software version upgrades (e.g., moving from Adobe ® 8.0 to 9.0), or changes to architecture (e.g., adding a new backup drive). The consideration is always about *how* this change to the baseline configuration is either a definite (standard) or negative (preferably, highly unlikely)?

It is crucial to describe the corporate RA process in terms of change needed and overall risk to the IT system. This should include who conducts the technical portion of the RA and who, in senior management, for example, the Chief Operating Officer (COO) or Chief Information Officer (CIO) that determines final approval.

MORE COMPLETE ANSWER: Implementing a more defined RA process could include standardized formats for RA artifacts. This could include a technical report written by knowledgeable IT personnel about a change, or a simplified form that allows for a checklist-like approach. It could also employ an outside third-party company that would formalize a review of the changes and their analysis of the overall impact of system security.

ASSESSMENT OBJECTIVE *Determine if:*		
SUB-CTRL	*DESCRIPTION*	**RECOMMENDED APPROACH**
3.11.1[a]	*The frequency to assess risk to organizational operations, organizational assets, and individuals are defined.*	NCR – (See discussion above regarding RA's conducted annually)

3.11.1[b]	Risk to organizational operations, organizational assets, and individuals resulting from the operation of an organizational system that processes, stores, or transmits CUI is assessed with the defined frequency.	NCR

ASSESSMENT METHODS AND CANDIDATE ARTIFACTS FOR REVIEW

Examine: [*SELECT FROM:* Risk assessment policy; security planning policy and procedures; procedures addressing organizational risk assessments; system security plan; risk assessment; risk assessment results; risk assessment reviews; risk assessment updates; other relevant documents or records].

Test: [*SELECT FROM:* Organizational processes for risk assessment; mechanisms supporting or for conducting, documenting, reviewing, disseminating, and updating the risk assessment].

Derived Security Requirements:

3.11.2 Scan for vulnerabilities in the information system and applications periodically and when new vulnerabilities affecting the system are identified.

MINIMUM ANSWER: This control requires that the company (system owner) regularly scans for vulnerabilities in the information system and hosted applications based upon a defined frequency or randomly based upon an established policy or procedure. This is also supposed to be applied when new vulnerabilities affecting the system or applications are identified.

The simplest way to address this control is by using **anti-virus** and **anti-malware** enterprise-levels of software versions. Major players in these areas include Symantec ®, McAfee ®, and Malwarebytes ®. Procedural documents should describe the products used to address "new vulnerabilities" using these solutions. See also SYSTEM AND INFORMATION INTEGRITY (SI) as a reinforcing control for this RA control.

MORE COMPLETE ANSWER: A suggested complete implementation could be the leveraging of company ISP services also is identified for providing a secondary layer of defense as a form of "trusted" connection. This could include any available SLA's that define the service provider's ability to mitigate such additional threats by employing **whitelisting** and **blacklisting** services; these services are designed to allow or restrict access depending on an **Access Control List** (ACL). See Control 3.14.2 for a more detailed description.

ASSESSMENT OBJECTIVE *Determine if:*		
SUB-CTRL	*DESCRIPTION*	**RECOMMENDED APPROACH**
3.11.2[a]	*The frequency to scan for vulnerabilities in organizational systems and applications is defined.*	NCR
3.11.2[b]	*Vulnerability scans are performed on organizational systems with the defined frequency.*	NCR
3.11.2[c]	*Vulnerability scans are performed on applications with the defined frequency.*	NCR – (typically monthly, but more often for major virus releases or "zero-day" threats)
3.11.2[d]	*Vulnerability scans are performed on organizational systems when new vulnerabilities are identified.*	NCR
3.11.2[e]	*Vulnerability scans are performed on applications when new vulnerabilities are identified.*	NCR

ASSESSMENT METHODS AND CANDIDATE ARTIFACTS FOR REVIEW

Examine: [*SELECT FROM:* Risk assessment policy; procedures addressing vulnerability scanning; risk assessment; system security plan; security assessment report; vulnerability scanning tools and associated configuration documentation; vulnerability scanning results; patch and vulnerability management records; other relevant documents or records].

Test: [*SELECT FROM:* Organizational processes for vulnerability scanning, analysis, remediation, and information sharing; mechanisms supporting or implementing vulnerability scanning, analysis, remediation, and information sharing].

3.11.3 Remediate vulnerabilities in accordance with assessments of risk.

MINIMUM ANSWER: Typically, anti-virus and anti-malware security applications cannot only detect but remove and quarantine malicious software. Update documentation accordingly.

This control also addresses "vulnerabilities" that are created by not meeting a specific control within the identified NIST 800-171 families. To address re-assessment activities, it is reasonable to update system POAM documentation with exact reasons any control is not met in full. This should attempt to answer what mitigation solutions are employed? When, by a specific date, the vulnerability will be corrected?

MORE COMPLETE ANSWER: Some additional means to better address this RA control is through other external services that can support ongoing remediation efforts. This could include the company's ISP or Cloud Service Providers. This could also include regular reviews of POAMs by both management and IT support staff personnel, for example, monthly or quarterly.

ASSESSMENT OBJECTIVE *Determine if:*		
SUB-CTRL	**DESCRIPTION**	**RECOMMENDED APPROACH**
3.11.3[a]	*Vulnerabilities are identified.*	NCR
3.11.3[b]	*Vulnerabilities are remediated in accordance with risk assessments.*	NCR

ASSESSMENT METHODS AND CANDIDATE ARTIFACTS FOR REVIEW

Examine: [*SELECT FROM:* Risk assessment policy; procedures addressing vulnerability scanning; risk assessment; system security plan; security assessment report; vulnerability scanning tools and associated configuration documentation; vulnerability scanning results; patch and vulnerability management records; other relevant documents or records].

Test: [*SELECT FROM:* Organizational processes for vulnerability scanning, analysis, remediation, and information sharing; mechanisms supporting or implementing vulnerability scanning, analysis, remediation, and information sharing].

SECURITY ASSESSMENT (SA)
Beginning Continuous Monitoring and Control Reviews

The SA control is about a process that re-assesses the state of all security controls and whether changes have occurred requiring additional mitigations of new risks or threats. The standard is 1/3rd of the controls are to be re-assessed annually. This would require designated IT personnel to conduct a SA event of approximately 36-37 controls per year. This should be captured in what is called a **ConMon Plan**. (See Appendix D, *CONTINUOUS MONITORING: A More Detailed Discussion* is an in-depth discussion of the current and future state of Continuous Monitoring and what it may mean to businesses).

Continuous Monitoring is a critical component of the NIST 800 series cybersecurity protection framework. It is defined as "...maintaining ongoing awareness of information security, vulnerabilities, and threats to support organizational risk management decisions," (NIST Special Publication 800-137, *Information Security Continuous Monitoring (ISCM) for Federal Information Systems and Organizations*,

http://nvlpubs.nist.gov/nistpubs/Legacy/SP/nistspecialpublication800-137.pdf).

ConMon is a significant guiding principle for the recurring execution of a Security Assessment.

Basic Security Requirements:

3.12.1 Periodically assess the security controls in organizational information systems to determine if the controls are effective in their application.

MINIMUM ANSWER: As described in the opening paragraph, meeting the basic requirements of the Security Assessment control should include the creation of a ConMon Plan and a review of 33% of the controls at least annually.

MORE COMPLETE ANSWER: A more thorough execution could include more than 33% of the controls being reviewed and reassessed; it is suggested to provide the results of annual Security Assessments to government contracting or their designated recipients.

ASSESSMENT OBJECTIVE *Determine if:*		
SUB-CTRL	*DESCRIPTION*	**RECOMMENDED APPROACH**
3.12.1[a]	*The frequency of security control assessments is defined.*	P- 1/3 of the controls should be assessed annually (typical)
3.12.1[b]	*Security controls are assessed with the defined frequency to determine if the controls are effective in their application.*	P-ConMon Plan will identify *"…Security controls … assessed with … defined frequency to determine if the controls are effective in their application."*
ASSESSMENT METHODS AND CANDIDATE ARTIFACTS FOR REVIEW Examine: [*SELECT FROM:* Security assessment and authorization policy; procedures addressing security assessment planning; procedures addressing security assessments; security assessment plan; system security plan; other relevant documents or records]. Test: [*SELECT FROM:* Mechanisms supporting security assessment, security assessment plan development, and security assessment reporting].		

3.12.2 Develop and implement plans of action designed to correct deficiencies and reduce or eliminate vulnerabilities in organizational information systems.

MINIMUM ANSWER: Where the security control is not fully implemented by the company or not recognized by the government as being fully compliant, a detailed POAM is necessary; review guidance under the AC control for a more detailed discussion of what is required in preparing a POAM for review.

As described earlier, this should include activities that are meant to answer the control in full or at least leverage other physical and virtual elements of other security controls to reinforce the posture of the control in question. A well-written POAM that is tracked and managed serves as the foundation for a reliable risk management process.

> *Cybersecurity is a leadership, not a technical challenge*

MORE COMPLETE ANSWER: Regular reviews by management and IT staff should enhance the company's cybersecurity posture. Cybersecurity is not just something that IT security personnel do; it includes the active oversight and review by corporate leadership to ensure effectiveness.

ASSESSMENT OBJECTIVE *Determine if:*		
SUB-CTRL	*DESCRIPTION*	**RECOMMENDED APPROACH**
3.12.2[a]	*Deficiencies and vulnerabilities to be addressed by the plan of action are identified.*	NCR – (The POAM)
3.12.2[b]	*A plan of action is developed to correct identified deficiencies and reduce or eliminate identified vulnerabilities.*	NCR
3.12.2[c]	*The plan of action is implemented to correct identified deficiencies and reduce or eliminate identified vulnerabilities.*	NCR

ASSESSMENT METHODS AND CANDIDATE ARTIFACTS FOR REVIEW
Examine: [*SELECT FROM:* Security assessment and authorization policy; procedures addressing plan of action; system security plan; security assessment plan; security assessment report; security assessment evidence; plan of action; other relevant documents or records].
Test: [*SELECT FROM:* Mechanisms for developing, implementing, and maintaining plan of action].

3.12.3 Monitor information system security controls on an ongoing basis to ensure the continued effectiveness of the controls.

MINIMUM ANSWER: This control can be answered in terms of a well-developed and executed ConMon Plan. Describing its purpose and the actions of assigned personnel to accomplish this task will answer this control.

MORE COMPLETE ANSWER: Suggested additional efforts regarding this control could include ad hoc spot checks of controls outside of the annual review process. Identify using the **PPT Model** described in Control 3.6.1 who is responsible for conducting the assessment (people), the workflow to adequately assess the current state of the control (process), and any supporting automation that provides feedback and reporting to management (technology).

3.12.4 Develop, document, and periodically update system security plans that describe system boundaries, system environments of operation, how security requirements are implemented, and the relationships with or connections to other systems.

MINIMUM ANSWER: this control requires that the **SSP** is updated regularly. The SSP should at a minimum be reviewed *annually* by designated company cybersecurity/IT personnel to ensure its accuracy. The SSP should be correctly updated sooner if there are significant changes to the:

- Hardware
- Software
- Network Architecture/Topology

MORE COMPLETE ANSWER: A more complete means to address this control is by addressing company change control boards. These are regular meetings when changes to hardware, software, or architecture occur. This should include mechanisms to document the occurrence of application and security patching. An effective procedure should always address changes to the IT system.

ASSESSMENT OBJECTIVE *Determine if:*		
SUB-CTRL	*DESCRIPTION*	**RECOMMENDED APPROACH**
3.12.4[a]	*A system security plan is developed.*	NCR – (The SSP)
3.12.4[b]	*The system boundary is described and documented in the system security plan.*	NCR (SSP)
3.12.4[c]	*The system environment of operation is described and documented in the system security plan.*	NCR (SSP)
3.12.4[d]	*The security requirements identified and approved by the designated authority as*	NCR (SSP)

	non-applicable are identified.	
3.12.4[e]	*The method of security requirement implementation is described and documented in the system security plan.*	NCR (SSP)
3.12.4[f]	*The relationship with or connection to other systems is described and documented in the system security plan.*	NCR (SSP) – This is specific to external systems such as telecommunications carriers or other servers (computers) accessed by the local IT environment to meet its mission requirements
3.12.4[g]	*The frequency to update the system security plan is defined.*	P-The SSP should be updated when significant or more accurately, "security-relevant" changes happen to the IT environment.
3.12.4[h]	*System security plan is updated with the defined frequency.*	P-While changes to the SSP should relate to significant changes for this sub-control we recommend an update at least every 90-180 days depending on the business or agencies complexity

ASSESSMENT METHODS AND CANDIDATE ARTIFACTS FOR REVIEW

<u>Examine</u>: [*SELECT FROM:* Security planning policy; procedures addressing system security plan development and implementation; procedures addressing system security plan reviews and updates; enterprise architecture documentation; system security plan; records of system security plan reviews and updates; other relevant documents or records].

<u>Test</u>: [*SELECT FROM:* Organizational processes for system security plan development, review, update, and approval; mechanisms supporting the system security plan].

Derived Security Requirements: None.

SYSTEM AND COMMUNICATIONS PROTECTION (SC)
External Communication and Connection Security

The overall risk management strategy is critical in establishing the appropriate technical solutions as well as procedural direction and guidance for the company. The core of this security control is that it establishes policy based upon applicable federal laws, Executive Orders, directives, regulations, policies, standards, and guidance. This control focuses on information security policy that can reflect the complexity of a business and its operation with the government. The procedures should be established for the security of the overall IT architecture and specifically for the components (hardware and software) of the information system.

In this control, many of the prior reinforcing controls can be used in demonstrating to the government a fuller understanding of NIST 800-171 requirements. The apparent repetition of other already developed technical solutions and procedural guides can be used as supporting these controls. However, it is crucial that corporate procedures are addressed individually— this is for traceability purposes of any potential current or future audit of the company's work by the government; clear and aligned explanations of the controls will make the approval process quicker.

Basic Security Requirements:

3.13.1 Monitor, control, and protect organizational communications (i.e., information transmitted or received by organizational information systems) at the external boundaries and essential internal boundaries of the information systems.

MINIMUM ANSWER: This control can be answered in the corporate procedure and include, for example, active auditing that checks for unauthorized access, individuals (external) who have had numerous failed logins, and traffic entering the network from "blacklisted" addresses, etc. The company should refer to its specific audit procedure as described in more detail under the AU control.

MORE COMPLETE ANSWER: This control could be better met as formerly discussed by using "smart" firewalls and advanced SIEM solutions. While costlier and requiring more considerable technical experience, corporate leadership should consider. These solutions, while not necessarily cost-effective for the current state of the company, it should be considered as part of any future architectural change effort. Any planning efforts should consider current and future technology purchases meant to enhance the cybersecurity posture of the company. See Appendix D for a broader description of SIEM technologies and how they may become part of the IT infrastructure.

ASSESSMENT OBJECTIVE *Determine if:*		
SUB-CTRL	*DESCRIPTION*	**RECOMMENDED APPROACH**
3.13.1[a]	*The external system boundary is defined.*	P/SSP-The "external system" boundary here is specific to firewalls and DMZ's. **This is part of the SSP.** This control also addresses protections, and this is only meant to identify where the "security boundary" is defined and known.
3.13.1[b]	*Key internal system boundaries are defined.*	SSP
3.13.1[c]	*Communications are monitored at the external system boundary.*	P- *"Communications are monitored at the external system boundary."*
3.13.1[d]	*Communications are monitored at key internal boundaries.*	P- *"Communications are monitored at key internal boundaries."*
3.13.1[e]	*Communications are controlled at the external system boundary.*	P- *"Communications are controlled at the external system boundary."*
3.13.1[f]	*Communications are controlled at key internal boundaries.*	P- *"Communications are controlled at key internal boundaries."*
3.13.1[g]	*Communications are protected at the external system boundary.*	P- *"Communications are protected at the external system boundary."*
3.13.1[h]	*Communications are protected at*	P- *"Communications are protected at key internal boundaries."*

key internal boundaries.	■ **This is where NIST 800-171A gets "granular" to a significant degree.**

ASSESSMENT METHODS AND CANDIDATE ARTIFACTS FOR REVIEW

Examine: [SELECT FROM: System and communications protection policy; procedures addressing boundary protection; system security plan; list of key internal boundaries of the system; system design documentation; boundary protection hardware and software; enterprise security architecture documentation; system audit logs and records; system configuration settings and associated documentation; other relevant documents or records].

Test: [SELECT FROM: Mechanisms implementing boundary protection capability].

3.13.2 Employ architectural designs, software development techniques, and systems engineering principles that promote effective information security within organizational information systems.

MINIMUM/MORE COMPLETE ANSWER: Describing effective security architectural design measures can be as simple as the employment of a properly configured firewall or 2FA/MFA utilized by the company. It is highly likely that the average company seeking contracts with the government will be specifically concerned with primary and secure architectures.

Other **mitigation** elements that can be described for this control may include physical security measures (e.g., a 24-hour guard force, reinforced fire doors, and cameras) or blacklist measures that prevent unauthorized applications from executing in the corporate network. See Control 3.13.10 for how 2FA operates internal or external to a company's network.

ASSESSMENT OBJECTIVE *Determine if:*		
SUB-CTRL	*DESCRIPTION*	**RECOMMENDED APPROACH**
3.13.2[a]	*Architectural designs that promote effective information security are identified.*	NCR/SSP-This includes firewalls, Intrusion Protection/Detection devices, etc.
3.13.2[b]	*Software development techniques that promote effective information security are identified.*	P- This requires that software development follows secure coding, scripting, etc., best practices, directions, and guidelines such as for DOD, Application Security Development (APPSECDEV) guidance.

3.13.2[c]	Systems engineering principles that promote effective information security are identified.	P- This requires that systems engineering follows secure engineering best practices.
3.13.2[d]	Identified architectural designs that promote effective information security are employed.	P- This requires that IT architecture and design follow secure engineering best practices.
3.13.2[e]	Identified software development techniques that promote effective information security are employed.	P- (See 3.13.2[b]) ■ Some of these control requirements may be reflected with third-party developers in the form of a contract.
3.13.2[f]	Identified systems engineering principles that promote effective information security are employed.	P- (See 3.13.2[c]) ■ Some of these control requirements may be reflected with third-party developers in the form of a contract.

ASSESSMENT METHODS AND CANDIDATE ARTIFACTS FOR REVIEW

Examine: [SELECT FROM: Security planning policy; procedures addressing system security plan development and implementation; procedures addressing system security plan reviews and updates; enterprise architecture documentation; system security plan; records of system security plan reviews and updates; system and communications protection policy; procedures addressing security engineering principles used in the specification, design, development, implementation, and modification of the system; security architecture documentation; security requirements and specifications for the system; system design documentation; system configuration settings and associated documentation; other relevant documents or records].

Test: [SELECT FROM: Organizational processes for system security plan development, review, update, and approval; mechanisms supporting the system security plan; processes for applying security engineering principles in system specification, design, development, implementation, and modification; automated mechanisms supporting the application of security engineering principles in information system specification, design, development, implementation, and modification].

Derived Security Requirements:

3.13.3 Separate user functionality from information system management functionality.

MINIMUM ANSWER: The policy should not allow privileged users to use the same credentials to access their user (e.g., email and Internet searches) and privileged user access. This separation of access is a basic network security principle and is intended to hamper both insider and external threats. (A suggested review of a similar control in Control 3.1.4, and its discussion of the **segregation of duties** principle for comparison.)

MORE COMPLETE ANSWER: There are technical solutions to automate this process. The product, for example, CyberArk ®, is used in many parts of the federal government to track and account for privileged user activity that is easily auditable. The ability to oversee especially privileged user activity should be readily audited and reviewed by senior company cybersecurity representatives.

ASSESSMENT OBJECTIVE *Determine if:*		
SUB-CTRL	*DESCRIPTION*	**RECOMMENDED APPROACH**
3.13.3[a]	*User functionality is identified.*	NCR
3.13.3[b]	*System management functionality is identified.*	NCR (This addresses functionalities such as System, Database Administrators, etc.)
3.13.3[c]	*User functionality is separated from system management functionality.*	NCR

POTENTIAL ASSESSMENT METHODS AND CANDIDATE ARTIFACTS FOR REVIEW
Examine: [*SELECT FROM:* System and communications protection policy; procedures addressing application partitioning; system design documentation; system configuration settings and associated documentation; system security plan; system audit logs and records; other relevant documents or records].
Test: [*SELECT FROM:* Separation of user functionality from system management functionality].

3.13.4 Prevent unauthorized and unintended information transfer via shared system resources.

MINIMUM ANSWER: **Peer-to-peer** networking is not authorized within many parts of the government, and it is strongly suggested the corporation's network also forbids its use. This is typically part of the AUP and should be enforceable to prevent, e.g., insider threat opportunities or used by external hackers to gain unauthorized access using legitimate employee security credentials.

MORE COMPLETE ANSWER: Suggest that this is part of the regular audit activity by designated IT personnel. They could be reviewing audit logs for unauthorized connections to include peer-to-peer networking.

3.13.5 Implement subnetworks for publicly accessible system components that are physically or logically separated from internal networks.

MINIMUM/MORE COMPLETE ANSWER: The most straightforward answer is that subnetworks reduce an intruder's ability to exploit corporate network addresses effectively. Have IT personnel establish subnetworks specifically for the email and webservers that are in the external Demilitarized Zone (DMZ) of the corporate's security boundary; see Control 3.14.2 for the location of a DMZ relative to the company's network. Some companies maintain external database servers; ensure they too have established subnetwork addresses.

ASSESSMENT OBJECTIVE *Determine if:*		
SUB-CTRL	*DESCRIPTION*	**RECOMMENDED APPROACH**
3.13.5[a]	*Publicly accessible system components are identified.*	NCR (Also should be part of SSP)
3.13.5[b]	*Subnetworks for publicly accessible system components are physically or logically separated from internal networks.*	NCR

ASSESSMENT METHODS AND CANDIDATE ARTIFACTS FOR REVIEW

Examine: [*SELECT FROM:* System and communications protection policy; procedures addressing boundary protection; system security plan; list of key internal boundaries of the system; system design documentation; boundary protection hardware and software; system configuration settings and associated documentation; enterprise security architecture documentation; system audit logs and records; other relevant documents or records].

Test: [*SELECT FROM:* Mechanisms implementing boundary protection capability].

3.13.6 Deny network communications traffic by default and allow network communications traffic by exception (i.e., deny all, permit by exception).

MINIMUM/MORE COMPLETE ANSWER: Like Control 3.4.8, this control can be selected by IT personnel. This is a technical control that should also be captured in the procedure document. These network settings are typically set at the firewall and involve **whitelisting** (only permitting access by exception) and **blacklisting** (from non-authorized Internet addresses) everyone else to enter the network. (Also, review Control 3.14.2.)

ASSESSMENT OBJECTIVE *Determine if:*		
SUB-CTRL	*DESCRIPTION*	**RECOMMENDED APPROACH**
3.13.6[a]	*Network communications traffic is denied by default.*	NCR
3.13.6[b]	*Network communications traffic is allowed by exception.*	NCR

ASSESSMENT METHODS AND CANDIDATE ARTIFACTS FOR REVIEW

Examine: [*SELECT FROM:* System and communications protection policy; procedures addressing boundary protection; system security plan; system design documentation; system configuration settings and associated documentation; system audit logs and records; other relevant documents or records].

Test: [*SELECT FROM:* Mechanisms implementing traffic management at managed interfaces].

3.13.7 Prevent remote devices from simultaneously establishing non-remote connections with the information system and communicating via some other connection to resources in external networks.

MINIMUM/MORE COMPLETE ANSWER: If a teleworking employee uses their remote device (i.e., notebook computer), and then connects to a non-remote (external) connection, it allows for an unauthorized external connection to exist; this provides a potential hacker with the ability to enter the network using the authorized employee's credentials.

It is critical that the company requires employees to use their VPN connection and blocks any unsecured connections from accessing internal systems or applications. IT personnel need to ensure these settings are correctly configured and are part of the corporate cybersecurity procedure documentation.

3.13.8 Implement cryptographic mechanisms to prevent unauthorized disclosure of CUI during transmission unless otherwise protected by alternative physical safeguards.

MINIMUM ANSWER: Remember, this control is about external communications from the network and its system boundary. This is a DIT issue and is protected by the cryptographic solutions discussed earlier; see Control 3.1.3. Documentation should reflect the type and level of protection of data transmitted. Any additional protections such as a VPN, a secure circuit/dedicated circuit provided by a commercially contracted carrier may afford more security for company data transmissions.

MORE COMPLETE ANSWER: Better levels of protection could be addressed regarding defense-in-depth, which is a current operational philosophy supported by the government; additional layers of security provide additional defense. (See the "Defense-in-Depth" diagram at Control 3.14.2).

ASSESSMENT OBJECTIVE *Determine if:*		
SUB-CTRL	*DESCRIPTION*	**RECOMMENDED APPROACH**
3.13.8[a]	*Cryptographic mechanisms intended to prevent unauthorized disclosure of CUI are identified.*	NCR
3.13.8[b]	*Alternative physical safeguards intended to prevent unauthorized disclosure of CUI are identified.*	NCR
3.13.8[c]	*Either cryptographic mechanisms or alternative physical safeguards are implemented to prevent unauthorized disclosure of CUI during transmission.*	NCR

POTENTIAL ASSESSMENT METHODS AND CANDIDATE ARTIFACTS FOR REVIEW

Examine: [*SELECT FROM:* System and communications protection policy; procedures addressing transmission confidentiality and integrity; system security plan; system design documentation; system configuration settings and associated documentation; system audit logs and records; other relevant documents or records].

Test: [*SELECT FROM:* Cryptographic mechanisms or mechanisms supporting or implementing transmission confidentiality; organizational processes for defining and implementing alternative physical safeguards].

3.13.9 Terminate network connections associated with communications sessions at the end of the sessions or after a defined period of inactivity.

MINIMUM ANSWER: This was addressed in the AC control specific to the complete termination of a session. Sessions of suggested importance would be those such as to the financial, HR, or other essential computer server systems housing defined CUI. It is recommended that the procedure is explicitly updated to this control re-using language provided by any response to the control(s) discussing the termination of a network connection.

MORE COMPLETE ANSWER: Audit of sessions that have timed-out can strengthen this control. SA's and IT staff can determine from audit logs that the prescribed time-out period was met and enforced. Provide a sampling to any inspector as part of the final packet.

ASSESSMENT OBJECTIVE *Determine if:*		
SUB-CTRL	*DESCRIPTION*	RECOMMENDED APPROACH
3.13.9[a]	*A period of inactivity to terminate network connections associated with communications sessions is defined.*	NCR
3.13.9[b]	*Network connections associated with communications sessions are terminated at the end of the sessions.*	NCR
3.13.9[c]	*Network connections associated with communications sessions are terminated after the defined period of inactivity.*	NCR
ASSESSMENT METHODS AND CANDIDATE ARTIFACTS FOR REVIEW		
Examine: [*SELECT FROM:* System and communications protection policy; procedures addressing network disconnect; system design documentation; system security plan; system configuration settings and associated documentation; system audit logs and records; other relevant documents or records].		
Test: [*SELECT FROM:* Mechanisms supporting or implementing network disconnect capability].		

3.13.10 Establish and manage cryptographic keys for cryptography employed in the information system.

MINIMUM ANSWER: There are two significant scenarios likely to occur:

1. Use of commercial cryptographic programs that resides within the company's architecture or is provided by an external "managed service" provider is the most likely scenarios. The keys will be maintained and secured by the cryptographic application. The company is establishing some form of 2FA solution. The public key would be secured somewhere else in the architecture, and the private key that of the employee would reside on a token such as CAC card or another critical device.

2. Using a 2FA solution with a CAC, Personal Identity Verification (PIV) card or "token" such as those produced by RSA ® is likely if the government authorizes the exchange of security keys on its systems with that of the company. This requires a Certificate Authority (CA) usually outside the local network either managed by the government or another trusted commercial entity with the capability to support "asymmetric" 2FA.

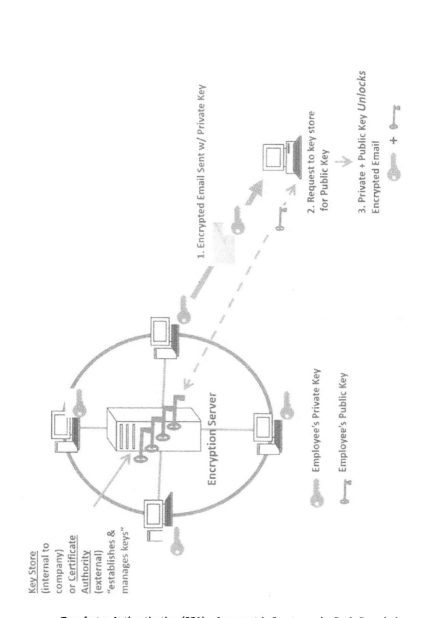

Two-factor Authentication (2FA) – Asymmetric Cryptography Basic Description

Whichever solution is used, ensure compatibility with government systems and other companies' as part of its normal operations. *All transmittal of CUI data is required to be encrypted.*

MORE COMPLETE ANSWER: Any more exceptional ability to secure and protect the **key store** within the company or through defined SLA's with outside service providers is essential. Ensure they have safeguards in place to protect unauthorized access to its system as well; they may use stronger encryption methods, but ensure they are recognized by the government and are Federal Information Processing Standards (FIPS 140-2) compliant. (See Control 3.13.11 for identifying FIPS 140-2 solutions).

ASSESSMENT OBJECTIVE *Determine if:*		
SUB-CTRL	*DESCRIPTION*	**RECOMMENDED APPROACH**
3.13.10[a]	*Cryptographic keys are established whenever cryptography is employed.*	NCR
3.13.10[b]	*Cryptographic keys are managed whenever cryptography is employed.*	NCR

ASSESSMENT METHODS AND CANDIDATE ARTIFACTS FOR REVIEW

Examine: [*SELECT FROM:* System and communications protection policy; procedures addressing cryptographic key establishment and management; system security plan; system design documentation; cryptographic mechanisms; system configuration settings and associated documentation; system audit logs and records; other relevant documents or records].

Test: [*SELECT FROM:* Mechanisms supporting or implementing cryptographic key establishment and management].

3.13.11 Employ FIPS-validated cryptography when used to protect the confidentiality of CUI.

MINIMUM/MORE COMPLETE ANSWER: The company needs to confirm that its encryption applications are FIPS 140-2 compliant. It can easily be verified at the website below:

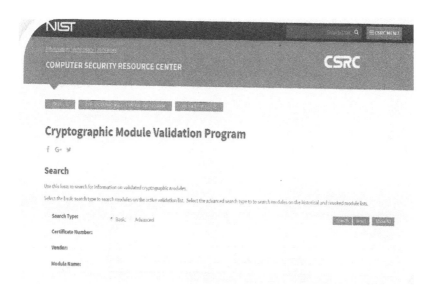

Official NIST site to confirm FIPS 140-2 cryptographic compliance
(https://csrc.nist.gov/projects/cryptographic-module-validation-program/validated-modules/search)

3.13.12 Prohibit remote activation of collaborative computing devices and indicate devices in use to users present at the device.

MINIMUM ANSWER: Collaborative computing devices include, for example, "networked whiteboards, cameras, and microphones." The intent is to prevent these devices from being used by intruders to conduct reconnaissance of a network.

This can be prevented by changes in registry settings that only authorized IT personnel with privileged access can change. Furthermore, if these items are active, visible lighting or audible alerts should be considered to notify IT and security personnel. The policy should require that individuals do not change these settings to include privileged users. Any change should only be approved by exception and require a privileged user who is authorized to make such changes.

MORE COMPLETE ANSWER: Auditing and SIEM solutions could be configured to ensure these settings are not tampered. See Control 3.3.2 for further discussion of this topic area.

ASSESSMENT OBJECTIVE *Determine if:*		
SUB-CTRL	*DESCRIPTION*	**RECOMMENDED APPROACH**
3.13.12[a]	*Collaborative computing devices are identified.*	NCR
3.13.12[b]	*Collaborative computing devices provide indication to users of devices in use.*	NCR
3.13.12[c]	*Remote activation of collaborative computing devices is prohibited.*	P - *"Remote activation of collaborative computing devices is prohibited."*

ASSESSMENT METHODS AND CANDIDATE ARTIFACTS FOR REVIEW

Examine: [*SELECT FROM:* System and communications protection policy; procedures addressing collaborative computing; access control policy and procedures; system security plan; system design documentation; system audit logs and records; system configuration settings and associated documentation; other relevant documents or records].

Test: [*SELECT FROM:* Mechanisms supporting or implementing management of remote activation of collaborative computing devices; mechanisms providing an indication of use of collaborative computing devices].

3.13.13 Control and monitor the use of mobile code.

MINIMUM/MORE COMPLETE ANSWER: Mobile code is mainly part of Internet-capable business phones. The company's phone carrier can limit the types and kinds of mobile applications that reside on employee phones. Most applications are usually required to meet secure industry development standards. It is best to confirm with the company's carrier how mobile code apps are secured and restrict employees to a set number of approved mobile apps. Define in the company procedures the base applications provided to each employee, and the process for work-specific applications that other specialists in the company require.

ASSESSMENT OBJECTIVE *Determine if:*		
SUB-CTRL	*DESCRIPTION*	**RECOMMENDED APPROACH**
3.13.13[a]	*Use of mobile code is controlled.*	P – *"Use of mobile code is controlled." (Restricted through a carrier and must be approved by the company or agency authorized representative before accessible by employees).*
3.13.13[b]	*Use of mobile code is monitored.*	P – *"Use of mobile code is monitored." (Reports provided on an established/contractual basis).*

3.13.14 Control and monitor the use of Voice over Internet Protocol (VoIP) technologies.

MINIMUM ANSWER: The most likely current place VOIP would exist is the company's phone service. Ensure with the phone carrier that their VOIP services are secure and what level of security is used to protect corporate communications. Furthermore, identify any contract information that provides details about the provided security.

MORE COMPLETE ANSWER: Verify what monitoring services and network protection (from malware, viruses, etc.) are part of the current service plan. If necessary, determine whether both the control and monitoring are included or extra services. If not fully included, consider formulating a POAM.

ASSESSMENT OBJECTIVE *Determine if:*		
SUB-CTRL	*DESCRIPTION*	**RECOMMENDED APPROACH**
3.13.14[a]	*Use of Voice over Internet Protocol (VoIP) technologies is controlled.*	NCR (See sub-control 3.13.13[a] for a similar discussion)
3.13.14[b]	*Use of Voice over Internet Protocol (VoIP) technologies is monitored.*	NCR

3.13.15 Protect the authenticity of communications sessions.

MINIMUM/ MORE COMPLETE ANSWER: This control addresses communications' protection and establishes confidence that the session is authentic; it ensures the identity of the individual and the information being transmitted. Authenticity protection includes, for example, protecting against session hijacking or insertion of false information.

This can be resolved by some form, hard or soft token MFA/2FA, solution. It will ensure the identity and FIPS 140-2 encryption to prevent data manipulation. See Control 3.5.2 for further discussion. While these are not ideal solutions, they significantly demonstrate more certainty that the communications are authentic.

3.13.16 Protect the confidentiality of CUI at rest.

MINIMUM ANSWER: This is a DAR issue, and as discussed earlier, it is a government requirement. Ensure the proper software package is procured that meets FIPS 140-2 standards. (See Control 3.13.11 for NIST's website information).

MORE COMPLETE ANSWER: If using a CSP, ensure it is using government accepted FIPS 140-2 standards; it will make authorization simpler. Moreover, a reminder, if the business cannot use FIPS 140-2 solutions, ensures an effective POAM is developed that addresses why it cannot be currently implemented and when the company is prepared to implement the control. *When will the company be compliant?*

SYSTEM AND INFORMATION INTEGRITY (SI)
Anti-virus and Anti-Malware

This control family is about maintaining the integrity of data within the company's system security boundary. It primarily defended by active measures such as anti-virus and malware protection. This control addresses the establishment of procedures for the effective implementation of the security controls. Cybersecurity policies and procedures may include Information Security (INFOSEC) policies. Company risk management strategy is a crucial factor in establishing decisive system protections.

Basic Security Requirements:

3.14.1 Identify, report, and correct information and information system flaws in a timely manner.

MINIMUM ANSWER: This control addresses what are considered security-relevant flaws. These would include, for example, software patches, hotfixes, anti-virus, and anti-malware signatures.

Typically, network Operating Systems can check with manufacturers via the Internet for updated, e.g., "security patches" in near-real-time. It is essential to allow patches from the authorized manufacturers and sources to be updated as soon as possible. They usually are designed to fix bugs and minor through significant security vulnerabilities. The sooner the system is updated, the better. Ensure a process, such as checks by IT personnel at least twice a day. Many systems will allow for automated "pushes" to the network. Ensure that documented processes account for review by IT personnel to "audit" known pushes by only authorized sources.

Major Security Events/Zero-Day Attacks: There are times that the State government becomes aware of **zero-day attacks**. These are attacks where there is no current security patch and sometimes requires other actions by government-supported organizations and corporations. Additionally, be aware of these events from the State as well as DOD and Department of Homeland Security (DHS). These will require near-immediate action. The AG, for example, may direct everyone, including NIST 800-171 authorized businesses, report their status by an established and compulsory deadline.

MORE COMPLETE ANSWER: Ensure that designated IT personnel are aware of and are monitoring the active vulnerabilities sites from the State of California, DOD, and DHS. An active process to verify the current state of threats against the government is an excellent means to establish a company's due diligence in this area.

DHS's United States Computer Emergency Readiness Team (US-CERT) has the latest information on vulnerabilities to include zero-day updates. It is also recommended that designated IT personnel sign up for the Rich Site Summary (RSS) data feeds by selecting the symbol to the left. The address for the overall site is: https://www.us-cert.gov/ncas/current-activity

---

ASSESSMENT OBJECTIVE *Determine if:*		
SUB-CTRL	*DESCRIPTION*	**RECOMMENDED APPROACH**
3.14.1[a]	*The time within which to identify system flaws is specified.*	P – Suggested: "Upon notification from X or upon the recognition that software patches or hotfixes are out of date; anti-virus and anti-malware signatures are not current, etc.
3.14.1[b]	*System flaws are identified within the specified time frame.*	P- This at a minimum should be upon recognition and a process that is in place to identify when reviews should occur, typically, weekly.
3.14.1[c]	*The time within which to report system flaws is specified.*	P – (See above)
3.14.1[d]	*System flaws are reported within the specified time frame.*	P – (See above)
3.14.1[e]	*The time within which to correct system flaws is specified.*	P- Flaws should be addressed immediately or within 24 hours, typically. Where a patch, for example, hurts operations, there need to be roll-back procedures. This should then require a POAM be documented with a possible waiver if the change is too negative.
3.14.1[f]	*System flaws are corrected within the specified time frame.*	P – (See 4.14.1[f])

3.14.2 Provide protection from malicious code at appropriate locations within organizational information systems.

MINIMUM ANSWER: Protecting the network from malicious code is typically through both active anti-virus and malware protection applications or services. Ensure if additional protections provided by the businesses' commercial ISP are included in any artifact submission.

MORE COMPLETE ANSWER: Any additional protections could be provided by "smart" firewalls, routers, and switches. Specific commercial devices provide extra defenses.

Smart Firewalls. Smart firewalls include standard protection capabilities. Additionally, firewalls specifically, can afford whitelisting and blacklisting protections.

- **Whitelisting** can be used only to allow authorized outside users on an internal Access Control List (ACL). The ACL needs to be managed actively to ensure that legitimate organizations can communicate through the businesses' firewall. The external interested business or organizations can still communicate with the business for some services like the company web site and email system that resides in what is termed the Demilitarized Zone (DMZ). Whitelisting is typically implemented at the firewall. See Diagram below.

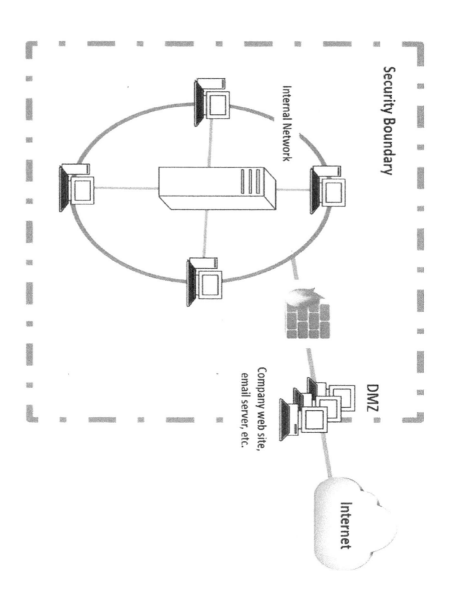

Basic Company Network View

- **Blacklisting** is used to block known "bad guys." There are companies and the government that can provide lists of known malicious sites based upon their Internet address. Blacklists require continuous management to be most effective.

Both solutions are not guaranteed. While they afford additional means to slow hackers and nation-state intruders, they are not total solutions. Therefore, the government, and much of the cybersecurity community, strongly supports the principle of **defense in depth** where other technological solutions help to reinforce the protections because of security programming flaws inadvertently created by software developers and the constant challenge of hackers exploiting various areas of modern IT architectures to conduct their nefarious actions.

The Principle of Defense in Depth

ASSESSMENT OBJECTIVE *Determine if:*		
SUB-CTRL	*DESCRIPTION*	**RECOMMENDED APPROACH**
3.14.2[a]	*Designated locations for malicious code protection are identified.*	P/SSP – Should identify the application and mechanisms within the architecture devoted to malicious code identification.
3.14.2[b]	*Protection from malicious code at designated locations is provided.*	P/SSP – (Same as 3.14.2[a])

POTENTIAL ASSESSMENT METHODS AND CANDIDATE ARTIFACTS FOR REVIEW

Examine: [*SELECT FROM:* System and information integrity policy; configuration management policy and procedures; procedures addressing malicious code protection; records of malicious code protection updates; malicious code protection mechanisms; system security plan; system configuration settings and associated documentation; record of actions initiated by malicious code protection mechanisms in response to malicious code detection; scan results from malicious code protection mechanisms; system design documentation; system audit logs and records; other relevant documents or records].

Test: [*SELECT FROM:* Organizational processes for employing, updating, and configuring malicious code protection mechanisms; organizational process for addressing false positives and resulting potential impact; mechanisms supporting or implementing employing, updating, and configuring malicious code protection mechanisms; mechanisms supporting or implementing malicious code scanning and subsequent actions].

3.14.3 Monitor information system security alerts and advisories and take appropriate actions in response.

MINIMUM ANSWER: This SI control can be best met through auditing. This can be met by using applications (such as anti-virus) or tools embedded within the architecture. These should include Intrusion Detection capabilities, network packet capture tools such as Wireshark ®, or audit logs. The process and associated actions should include recognition and notification to senior management. Management should ensure developed processes define when an event is raised to a level of a notifiable incident to the government.

MORE COMPLETE ANSWER: A more-complete solution could use other advanced toolsets based on the education and experience of the IT support staff. These could include malicious code protection software (such as found in more advanced anti-malware solutions). Consideration should always include the overall ROI for the investment in such tools.

If the company can only implement minor portions of the control and has the planned intent to invest in improved tools in the future, it is best to develop a well-defined POAM with achievable milestones for the company to pursue. It will demonstrate to the US government a commitment to improving cybersecurity vice ignoring other technical methods to reduce the risk to the company and its associated CUI.

ASSESSMENT OBJECTIVE *Determine if:*		
SUB-CTRL	**DESCRIPTION**	**RECOMMENDED APPROACH**
3.14.3[a]	*Response actions to system security alerts and advisories are identified.*	P – This would align with the Incident Response Plan (IRP); (See IR 3.6 Controls)
3.14.3[b]	*System security alerts and advisories are monitored.*	P – This would identify who monitors; small companies may include SA's and larger companies with use their Security Operations Center (SOC) watch personnel
3.14.3[c]	*Actions in response to system security alerts and advisories are taken.*	P – Part of IRP and designated personnel.

POTENTIAL ASSESSMENT METHODS AND CANDIDATE ARTIFACTS FOR REVIEW
Examine: [*SELECT FROM:* System and information integrity policy; procedures addressing security alerts, advisories, and directives; system security plan; records of security alerts and advisories; other relevant documents or records].
Test: [*SELECT FROM:* Organizational processes for defining, receiving, generating, disseminating, and complying with security alerts, advisories, and directives; mechanisms supporting or implementing definition, receipt, generation, and dissemination of security alerts, advisories, and directives; mechanisms supporting or implementing security directives].

Derived Security Requirements:

3.14.4 Update malicious code protection mechanisms when new releases are available.
MINIMUM/COMPLETE ANSWER: This is usually quickly resolved through ongoing software license agreements with vendors for malicious code internal programs or external contracted support services. Assuming a new version is made available during the active period of the license, updates are typically free; document the company's procedure for maintaining not only current but legal versions of malicious code detection and prevention software or services.

3.14.5 Perform periodic scans of the information system and real-time scans of files from external sources as files are downloaded, opened, or executed.

MINIMUM ANSWER: Many of the solutions already discussed afford real-time scanning of files and traffic as they traverse the network. Scanning of files should always be conducted from external downloads for both viruses and malware. Ensure the technical policy settings are always set to conduct real-time scans of the network, endpoints (i.e., work computers both internal and used by teleworking employees), and files entering the network by the appropriate tools to ensure network operation and security.

MORE COMPLETE ANSWER: Require IT personnel to regularly check that real-time scanning has not been changed accidentally or on purpose. It is essential to be aware that potential intruders will attempt to shut down any security features such as active scanning. Train IT personnel to manually check at least weekly and alert management if the changes are suspicious. Identifying possible entry into the company's data is a function of the SI as well as a significant component of the AU control family.

ASSESSMENT OBJECTIVE *Determine if:*		
SUB-CTRL	*DESCRIPTION*	**RECOMMENDED APPROACH**
3.14.5[a]	*The frequency for malicious code scans is defined.*	NCR – Recommended: real-time using approved malware detection software; otherwise, at least daily for smaller operations (not recommended until the tool is purchased and deployed)
3.14.5[b]	*Malicious code scans are performed with the defined frequency.*	NCR
3.14.5[c]	*Real-time malicious code scans of files from external sources as files are downloaded, opened, or executed are performed.*	NCR

3.14.6 Monitor the information system including inbound and outbound communications traffic, to detect attacks and indicators of potential attacks.

MINIMUM ANSWER: As discussed, anti-virus and malware provide some level of checking of inbound and outbound traffic. Document both manual and automated means to ensure traffic is monitored.

Procedures should identify the people who will conduct the regular review, the process that ensures proper oversight is in place to identify violations of this control, and what technologies are being used to protect inbound and outbound traffic from attack. (See Control 3.6.1 for discussion about the PPT Model, and its application to address security controls).

MORE COMPLETE ANSWER: This could also identify commercial ISP's supporting the business with "trusted" connections to the Internet. Refer to provided SLA's and contract information for government review.

ASSESSMENT OBJECTIVE *Determine if:*		
SUB-CTRL	*DESCRIPTION*	**RECOMMENDED APPROACH**
3.14.6[a]	*The system is monitored to detect attacks and indicators of potential attacks.*	NCR
3.14.6[b]	*Inbound communications traffic is monitored to detect attacks and indicators of potential attacks.*	NCR

3.14.6[c]	Outbound communications traffic is monitored to detect attacks and indicators of potential attacks.	NCR

ASSESSMENT METHODS AND CANDIDATE ARTIFACTS FOR REVIEW

Examine: [*SELECT FROM:* System and information integrity policy; procedures addressing system monitoring tools and techniques; continuous monitoring strategy; system and information integrity policy; procedures addressing system monitoring tools and techniques; facility diagram or layout; system security plan; system monitoring tools and techniques documentation; system design documentation; locations within system where monitoring devices are deployed; system protocols; system configuration settings and associated documentation; system audit logs and records; other relevant documents or records].

Test: [*SELECT FROM:* Organizational processes for system monitoring; mechanisms supporting or implementing intrusion detection capability and system monitoring; mechanisms supporting or implementing system monitoring capability; organizational processes for intrusion detection and system monitoring; mechanisms supporting or implementing the monitoring of inbound and outbound communications traffic].

3.14.7 Identify unauthorized use of the information system.

MINIMUM ANSWER: This is met through active and regular auditing of, for example, systems, applications, intrusion detections, and firewall logs. It is essential to recognize that there may be limitations for the IT staff to properly and adequately review all available logs created by the company's IT network. It is best to identify the critical logs to review regularly and any secondary logs as time permits. Avoid trying to review all available system logs; there are many. Also, determine the level of effort, required processing time, ability, and training of the company's' IT support staff.

MORE COMPLETE ANSWER: In addition to the above, consider third-party companies that can provide a monitoring service of the network. While these may be expensive, it will depend on the business, its mission, and the critically of the data. This solution will require a well-developed SLA's with appropriate oversight to ensure the company receives the Quality of Service (QOS) the company needs.

ASSESSMENT OBJECTIVE *Determine if:*		
SUB-CTRL	*DESCRIPTION*	**RECOMMENDED APPROACH**
3.14.7[a]	*Authorized use of the system is defined.*	NCR
3.14.7[b]	*Unauthorized use of the system is identified.*	NCR

ASSESSMENT METHODS AND CANDIDATE ARTIFACTS FOR REVIEW

Examine: [SELECT FROM: Continuous monitoring strategy; system and information integrity policy; procedures addressing system monitoring tools and techniques; facility diagram/layout; system security plan; system design documentation; system monitoring tools and techniques documentation; locations within system where monitoring devices are deployed; system configuration settings and associated documentation; other relevant documents or records].

Test: [SELECT FROM: Organizational processes for system monitoring; mechanisms supporting or implementing system monitoring capability].

CONCLUSION
This is Risk Management, NOT Risk Elimination

The major premise of the NIST cybersecurity process is to recognize that it is not about the absolute certainty that the security controls will stop every type of cyber-attack and protect the consumer's data. Risk Management is about recognizing the system's overall weaknesses through the RMF process, using POAMs to manage the risks, and being continually monitoring the threats to the IT environment. It is about the company's leadership, not just the IT staff, has identified where those weaknesses exist and have created plans to, at a minimum, mitigate the success of a would-be cyber-attacker.

Risk Management is about a defined Continuous Monitoring (ConMon) and effective Risk Assessment processes. Such processes afford the needed protection to secure private consumer information. These are not meant to be complete answers to an ever-changing risk landscape. It is only through an active and continual review of the controls can the Federal or State government, and companies ensure near-certainty their networks are as secure *as possible.*

A crucial final objective of this book is to provide a plain-English and how-to guide for the non-IT business owner in their application of California's CCPA. The target of this book is to provide information that they and their IT staffs can critically think about and how to best respond to these 110 security controls. This book provides a useful roadmap for small through big businesses to not only meet the requirements of NIST 800-171, NOT JUST FOR CCPA, but to truly protect their computers, systems, and especially the personal information of its customers from the "bad guys" near and far.

APPENDIX A – Relevant Terms & Glossary

Audit log.	A chronological record of information system activities, including records of system accesses and operations performed in each period.
Authentication.	Verifying the identity of a user, process, or device, often as a prerequisite to allowing access to resources in an information system.
Availability.	Ensuring timely and reliable access to and use of information.
Baseline Configuration.	A documented set of specifications for an information system, or a configuration item within a system, that has been formally reviewed and agreed on at a given point in time, and which can be changed only through change control procedures.
Blacklisting.	The process used to identify: (i) software programs that are not authorized to execute on an information system; or (ii) prohibited websites.
Confidentiality.	Preserving authorized restrictions on information access and disclosure, including means for protecting personal privacy and proprietary information.
Configuration Management.	A collection of activities focused on establishing and maintaining the integrity of information technology products and information systems, through control of processes for initializing, changing, and monitoring the configurations of those products and systems throughout the system development life cycle.
Controlled Unclassified Information (CUI).	
	Information that law, regulation, or governmentwide policy requires to have safeguarding or disseminating controls, excluding information that is classified under Executive Order 13526, Classified National Security Information, December 29, 2009, or any predecessor or successor order, or the Atomic Energy Act of 1954, as amended.
External network.	A network not controlled by the company.
FIPS-validated cryptography.	A cryptographic module validated by the Cryptographic Module Validation Program (CMVP) to meet requirements specified in FIPS Publication 140-2 (as amended). As a prerequisite to CMVP validation,

the cryptographic module is required to employ a cryptographic algorithm implementation that has successfully passed validation testing by the Cryptographic Algorithm Validation Program (CAVP).

Hardware.   The physical components of an information system.

Incident.   An occurrence that actually or potentially jeopardizes the confidentiality, integrity, or availability of an information system or the information the system processes, stores, or transmits or that constitutes a violation or imminent threat of violation of security policies, security procedures, or acceptable use policies.

Information Security.   The protection of information and information systems from unauthorized access, use, disclosure, disruption, modification, or destruction to provide confidentiality, integrity, and availability.

Information System.   A discrete set of information resources organized for the collection, processing, maintenance, use, sharing, dissemination, or disposition of information.

Information Technology.   Any equipment or interconnected system or subsystem of equipment that is used in the automatic acquisition, storage, manipulation, management, movement, control, display, switching, interchange, transmission, or reception of data or information by the executive agency. It includes computers, ancillary equipment, software, firmware, and similar procedures, services (including support services), and related resources.

Integrity.   Guarding against improper information modification or destruction and includes ensuring information non-repudiation and authenticity.

Internal Network.   A network where: (i) the establishment, maintenance, and provisioning of security controls are under the direct control of organizational employees or contractors; or (ii) cryptographic encapsulation or similar security technology implemented between organization-controlled endpoints, provides the same effect (at least concerning confidentiality and integrity).

Malicious Code.   Software intended to perform an unauthorized process that will hurt the confidentiality, integrity, or availability of an information system. A virus, worm, Trojan horse, or other code-based entity infects a host computer or system. Spyware and some forms of adware are also examples of malicious code.

Media.	Physical devices or writing surfaces including, but not limited to, magnetic tapes, optical disks, magnetic disks, and printouts (but not including display media) onto which information is recorded, stored, or printed within an information system.
Mobile Code.	Software programs or parts of programs obtained from remote information systems, transmitted across a network, and executed on a local information system without explicit installation or execution by the recipient.
Mobile device.	A portable computing device that: (i) has a small form factor such that a single individual can easily carry it; (ii) is designed to operate without a physical connection (e.g., wirelessly transmit or receive information); (iii) possesses local, nonremovable or removable data storage; and (iv) includes a self-contained power source. Mobile devices may also include voice communication capabilities, on-board sensors that allow the devices to capture information or built-in features for synchronizing local data with remote locations. Examples include smartphones, tablets, and E-readers.
Multifactor Authentication.	Authentication using two or more different factors to achieve authentication. Factors include: (i) something you know (e.g., password/PIN); (ii) something you have (e.g., cryptographic identification device, token); or (iii) something you are (e.g., biometric).
Nonfederal Information System.	An information system that does not meet the criteria for a federal information system. Nonfederal organization.
Network.	Information system(s) implemented with a collection of interconnected components. Such components may include routers, hubs, cabling, telecommunications controllers, key distribution centers, and technical control devices.
Portable storage device.	An information system component that can be inserted into and removed from an information system, and that is used to store data or information (e.g., text, video, audio, or image data). Such components are typically implemented on magnetic, optical, or solid-state devices (e.g., floppy disks, compact/digital video disks, flash/thumb drives, external hard disk drives, and flash memory cards/drives that contain nonvolatile memory).
Privileged Account.	An information system account with authorizations of a privileged user.

Privileged User.	A user that is authorized (and therefore, trusted) to perform security-relevant functions that ordinary users are not authorized to perform.
Remote Access.	Access to an organizational information system by a user (or a process acting on behalf of a user) communicating through an external network (e.g., the Internet).
Risk.	A measure of the extent to which a potential circumstance or event threaten an entity, and typically a function of (i) the adverse impacts that would arise if the circumstance or event occurs; and (ii) the likelihood of occurrence. Information system-related security risks are those risks that arise from the loss of confidentiality, integrity, or availability of information or information systems and reflect the potential adverse impacts to organizational operations (including mission, functions, image, or reputation), organizational assets, individuals, other organizations, and the Nation.
Sanitization.	Actions taken to render data written on media unrecoverable by both ordinary and, for some forms of sanitization, extraordinary means. The process to remove information from media such that data recovery is not possible. It includes removing all classified labels, markings, and activity logs.
Security Control.	A safeguard or countermeasure prescribed for an information system or an organization designed to protect the confidentiality, integrity, and availability of its information and to meet a set of defined security requirements.
Security Control Assessment.	The testing or evaluation of security controls to determine the extent to which the controls are implemented correctly, operating as intended, and producing the desired outcome for meeting the security requirements for an information system or organization.
Security Functions.	The hardware, software, or firmware of the information system responsible for enforcing the system security policy and supporting the isolation of code and data on which the protection is based.
Threat.	Any circumstance or event with the potential to adversely impact organizational operations (including mission, functions, image, or reputation), organizational assets, individuals, other organizations, or the Nation through an information system via unauthorized access, destruction, disclosure, modification of information, or denial of service.

Whitelisting.   The process used to identify: (i) software programs that are authorized to execute on an information system.

APPENDIX B – Managing the Lifecycle of a POAM

This section is designed to suggest a structure and approach for anyone developing a POAM for their company or agency. It describes how to address the POAM development process and how to formulate and track POAMs during their lifecycle. We suggest using the US Intelligence Community's *Intelligence Lifecycle* as a guide to address POAM's from "cradle-to-grave." The process has been slightly modified to provide a more pertinent description for POAM creation, but we have found this model to be useful for the novice through professional cybersecurity or IT specialist that regularly works in this arena.

This includes the following six stages:

1. **IDENTIFY:** Those controls that time, technology, or cost cannot be met to satisfy the unimplemented control.

2. **RESEARCH:** You now have decided the control is not going to meet your immediate NIST 800-171 needs. The typical initial milestone is to conduct some form of research or market survey of available solutions. This will include:

   - **The kind or type of solution.** Either as a person (e.g., additional expertise), process (e.g., what established workflow can provide a repeatable solution) or technology (e.g., what hardware/software solution fixes all or part of the control.

   - **How the State government wants it implemented**? For example, are hard tokens required, or can the company use some form of soft token solution to address 2FA?

   - **Internal challenges.** What does the company face overall with people, process, or technology perspectives specific to the control?

3. **RECOMMEND:** At this phase, all research and analysis has been completed, and presumably well-documented. Typically, the cybersecurity team or business IT team will formulate recommended solutions to the System Owner, i.e., the business decision-makers such as the Chief Information or Operations Officer. The recommendations must not only be technically feasible, but cost and resources should be part of any recommendation.

4. **DECIDE:** At this point, company decision-makers not only approve of the approach to correct the security shortfall but have agreed to resource requirements to authorize the expenditures of funds and efforts.

5. **IMPLEMENT:** Finally, the solution is implemented, and the POAM is updated for closure. This should be reported to the Contract Office or its representative regularly.

6. **CONTINUAL IMPROVEMENT.** Like any process, it should be regularly reviewed and updated accurately to the needs and capabilities of the company or organization. This could include better templates, additional staffing, or more regular updates to management to ensure both a thorough but supportive understanding of how cybersecurity meets the needs and mission of the business.

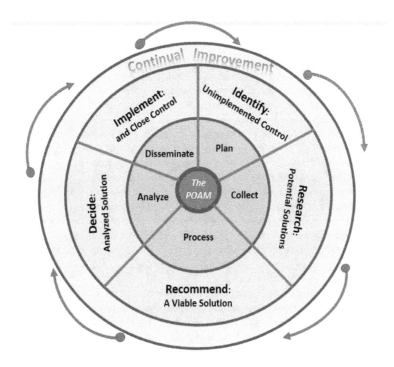

The POAM Lifecycle

We begin in the "Identify" section of the lifecycle process above. At this stage, several things may occur. Either the business owner or IT staff recognizes that the security control is not or cannot be immediately met, or they employ an automated security tool, such as ACAS® or Nessus®, that identifies securities vulnerabilities within the information system. This could also include findings such as the default password, like "password," has not been changed on an internal switch or router. It could also include updated security patching has not occurred;

some automated application scanning tools will not only identify but recommend courses of action to mitigate or fix a security finding. Always try to leverage those as soon as possible to secure the IT environment.

Also, assumed in this stage is the act of documenting findings. The finding should be placed in a POAM template as the business moves through the lifecycle. This could be done using documents created in Word®, for example, but we recommend using a spreadsheet program that allows for the easier filtering and management of the POAM. Spreadsheets afford greater flexibility during the "heavy lift" portion of formulating all POAMs not intended to be fixed immediately because of technical shortfalls. This may include not having in-house technical expertise, for example, to setup Two Factor Authentication (2FA) or because of current company financial limitations; this would most likely be reasonable when the costs are currently prohibitive to implement a specific control.

In the "research" phase, this includes technical analysis, Internet searches, market research, etc., regarding viable solutions to address the security control not being "compliant." This activity is typically part of an initial milestone established in the POAM. It may be added in the POAM, and could be, for example: "Conduct initial market research of candidate systems that can provide an affordable Two Factor Authentication (2FA) solution to meet security control 3.X.X." Another example might be: "The cybersecurity section will identify at least two candidate Data at Rest (DAR) solutions to protect the company's corporate and CUI data." These initial milestones are a normal part of any initial milestones that clearly describes reasonable actions to address non-complaint controls.

Another part of any milestone establishment action is to identify when a milestone is expected to be complete. Typically, milestones are done for 30 days, but if the complexity of such an activity requires additional time, ensure the company as identified reasonable periods of times with actual dates of *expected* completion. Never use undefined milestones such as "next version update" or "Calendar Year 2020 in Quarter 4." Real dates are mandatory to indeed manage findings supported by, for example, automated workflow or tracking applications the company may acquire in the future to enhance its cybersecurity risk management program.

At the "recommendation" phase, this is the time when the prior research has resulted in at least one solution, be it additional skilled personnel (people), enhanced company policies that manage the security control better (process), or a device that solves the control in part or total (technology). This should be part of this phase and be part of the POAM template as a milestone with the expected completion date.

At the "decide" phase, company or agency decision-makers should approve a recommended solution, and that decision should be documented in a configuration change tracking document, configuration management decision memorandum or in the POAM itself. This should include approved resources, but most importantly, any funding decision should be acted upon as quickly as possible. While many of these suggestions may seem necessary, it is often overlooked to document the decision so future personnel and management can understand how the solution was determined.

The "implementation" phase may become the most difficult. It is where a leader should be designated to coordinate the specific activity to meet the control— it may not necessarily be a technical solution, but may also include, for example, a documentation development activity that creates a process to manage the POAM.

Implementation should also include primary programmatic considerations. This should include performance, schedule, cost, and risk:

- Performance: consider what success the solution is attempting to address. Can it send email alerts to users? Will the system shutdown automatically once an intrusion is confirmed in the corporate network? Will the Incident Response Plan include notifications to law enforcement? Performance is always a significant and measurable means to ensure that the solution will address the POAM/security control shortfall. Always try to measure performance specific to the actual control that is being met.

- Schedule: Devise a plan based upon the developed milestones that are reasonable and not unrealistic. As soon as a deviation becomes apparent, ensure that the POAM template is updated and approved by management. This should be a senior management representative with authority to provide extensions to the current plan. This could include, for example, a Senior IT Manager, Chief Information Security Officer, or Chief Operating Officer.

- Cost: While it is assumed that all funding has been provided early in the process, always ensure contingencies are in place to request additional funding. It is common in most IT programs to maintain a 15-20% funding reserve for emergencies. Otherwise, the Project Manager or lead will have to re-justify to management for additional funding late in the implementation portion of the cycle.

- Risk: This is not the risk identified, for example, by the review of security controls or automated scans of the system. This risk is specific to the program's success to accomplish its goal to close the security finding. Risk should always be focus on the performance, cost, and schedule risks as significant concerns. Consider creating a risk matrix or risk log to help during the implementation phase.

Finally, ensure that as soon as the company can satisfactorily implement its solution close the control and notify the Contract Office of the completion. Typically, updates and notifications should occur at least once a quarter, but more often is appropriate for more highly impactful controls. Two-factor authentication and automated auditing, for example, are best updated as quickly as possible. This not only secures the company's network and IT environment but builds confidence with the government that security requirements are being met.

A final area to consider in terms of best-practices within cybersecurity, and more specifically in developing complete POAMs, is the area of **continual improvement**. Leveraging the legacy Intelligence Lifecycle process should be an ongoing model for IT and cybersecurity specialists to emulate. Those supporting this process should always be prepared to make changes or modifications that better represent the state and readiness of the system with its listing of POAMs. The Intelligence

Lifecycle provides the ideal model for a business to follow and implement to meet its POAM responsibilities within NIST 800-171.

 For the technically-capable company: Consider importing POAM spreadsheets into a database program and using its internal reporting creation and report capabilities. It can be used to enhance POAM status reporting and tracking for Senior Management.

CUI Protection Measures[18]

Security markings and safeguarding is a major part of being successful in the application of NIST 800-171. Proper marking is not just for the company or agency, but for those not intended or authorized to view CUI. This chapter delineates how to mark all forms of written and electronic media in order to protect sensitive CUI. While it is unlikely a company or business will create CUI, it will be responsible for the legal protections from either administrative, civil, or criminal implications of failing to properly care for CUI. **Do not be careless.**

The CUI Program standardizes how the Executive branch handles unclassified information[19] that does not meet the criteria required for classification under E.O. 13526, "Classified National Security Information," December 29, 2009, or the Atomic Energy Act but must be protected based on law, regulation, or Government-wide policy. Protections involve the safeguards employed while this information is stored or handled by the Executive branch departments or its subordinate agencies.

Before implementation of the CUI Program, agencies employed *ad hoc*, agency-specific policies, procedures, and markings to safeguard and control this information. This information involved privacy, security, proprietary business interests, and law enforcement information. This was highly inefficient and confusing. Subsequent guidance resulted in inconsistent marking and safeguarding of documents that led to unclear or unnecessarily restrictive dissemination policies. Furthermore, it created obstacles to the *best practice* principle of *Information Sharing,* resulting in part from the 9-11 attack of September 11, 2001[20].

Proper markings alert information holders to the presence of CUI and subsequently when portion markings are required. Markings ensure that CUI is identified and the exact information is appropriately marked for protection. They alert CUI holders to any dissemination and

---

[18] This chapter is adapted from the National Archives and Records Administration (NARA) information and artifacts regarding the national CUI program.

[19] While the Legislative and Judicial Branch should defer to the Executive Branch for all matters regarding national security protections and markings, it cannot be guaranteed for vendors working with the other two branches of the US government.

[20] One of the major findings of the 9-11 Commission was that the Central Intelligence Agency (CIA) and the Federal Bureau of Investigation (FBI) each had pieces of critical intelligence that may have prevented the attacks. Congress mandated created information sharing efforts—however, the parochial nature of government has not as of yet solved this problem.

safeguarding controls. This chapter provides basic marking guidelines for CUI and is written to provide visibility and requisite security to CUI.

Companies, businesses, organizations, agencies, and most specifically, employees must review their organizations CUI policy before marking any CUI. The handling of CUI must be per **E.O. 13556, "Controlled Unclassified Information," November 4, 2010**, 32 CFR Part 2002 (this link provides a full version https://www.govinfo.gov/content/pkg/CFR-2017-title32-vol6/pdf/CFR-2017-title32-vol6-part2002.pdf) , supplemental guidance published by the government's overall CUI Executive Agent (EA), the National Archive and Records Administration (NARA), and all applicable EA-approved agency policies. This chapter contains guidance on what each marking is, where and how to apply it, and which items are mandatory or optional based on local agency or organization policy.

CUI Banner Markings (Reference 32 CFR 2002.20(b))

Banner markings are the necessary header (and footer) designations alerting individuals with a need-to-know the required restrictions in place to ensure the protection of the information. Banner makings should be seen by individuals to ensure the maximum protection if the information is set out in the open or inadvertently visible to unauthorized individuals. Those individuals charged with the protection of the CUI are administratively responsible for CUI and protection and are subject to disciplinary actions by the agency or company. The following is a list of basic knowledge required by the agency as well as recipient vendors and contractors of the US Government.

- The initial marking for all CUI is the CUI Banner Marking. This is the central marking that appears at the top (and typically, at the bottom) of each page of any document that contains CUI.

- This marking is MANDATORY for all documents containing CUI. The content of the CUI Banner Marking must be inclusive of all CUI within the document and must be the same on each page.

- The Banner Marking should appear as bold capitalized black text and be centered when feasible. (*There are no designated size or font requirements, but we recommend the same font used for the document, and at least four sizes larger for visual prominence*).

- The CUI Banner Marking may include up to three elements:

    1. The CUI Control Marking (mandatory) may consist of either the

word "CONTROLLED" or the acronym "CUI."

2. CUI Category or Subcategory Markings (mandatory for CUI Specified). These are separated from the CUI Control Marking by a double forward-slash (//). When including multiple categories or subcategories in a Banner Marking, they must be alphabetized and are separated by a single forward-slash (/).

3. Limited Dissemination (LIMDIS) Control Markings are preceded by a double forward-slash (//) to separate them from the rest of the CUI Banner Marking.

A sample of the CUI Banner Marking may be found below.

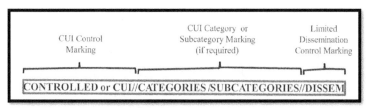

CUI Banner Marking

The above example uses the words "CATEGORIES" and "SUBCATEGORIES" as substitutes for CUI Category or Subcategory Markings and the word "DISSEM" as a substitute for Limited Dissemination Control Marking. Consult the CUI Registry for actual CUI markings.

CUI Banner Control Markings (Reference 32 CFR 2002.20(b)(1))

The CUI Control Marking is mandatory for all CUI and may consist of either the word "CONTROLLED" or the acronym "CUI" (at the designator's discretion). A best practice for CUI Banner Marking includes it being placed at the bottom of the document. Below are two examples showing the options for the CUI Banner Marking.

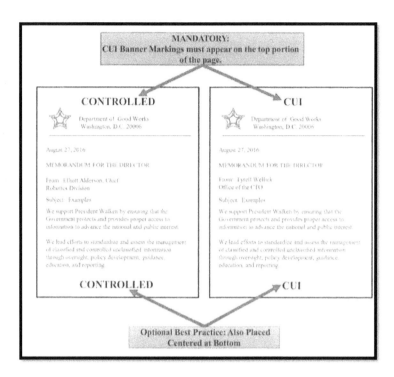

CUI Categories and Subcategories (Reference 32 CFR 2002.12)

The CUI Program is founded on the precondition that only information requiring protection based on law, Federal regulation, or government-widepolicy can qualify as CUI. *CUI Categories and Subcategories are necessarily different*. CUI Categories and Subcategories are based on at least one or more laws, regulations, or government-wide policies; these are also referred to as *Authorities*[21] that require a specific type of information be protected or restricted in its dissemination.

There are two types of CUI Categories and Subcategories: CUI Basic and CUI Specified.

---

[21] Consider Authorities as local rules or policies that are unique to the particular Federal agency. Typically, the Contract Officer should be able to assist in information briefings with the agency to ensure full compliance by the vendor.

1. ***CUI Basic*** is the standard CUI category. All rules of CUI apply to CUI Basic Categories and Subcategories. This ensures the proper creation and handling of properly marked CUI.

2. ***CUI Specified*** is different since the requirements for how users must treat each type of information vary with each Category or Subcategory. This is because some Authorities have specialized requirements for handling varied types of CUI information.

CUI Specified is NOT a "higher level" of CUI, it is *merely different*. Also, its differences are dictated by law, Federal regulation, or government-wide policy; they cannot be ignored. Furthermore, a document containing multiple CUI Specified Categories and Subcategories must include all of them in the CUI Banner Marking.

There is one additional issue with CUI Specified. Some CUI Categories and Subcategories are only CUI Specified sometimes based upon the Authorities local rules or policies. The reason these differences are caused by differing laws or regulations about the same information type; however, only *some* of them may include additional or alternate handling requirements for standard CUI Basic.

Therefore, only CUI created under Authorities would be CUI Specified. Explicitly, if the law, regulation, or Government-wide policy that pertains to an agency are listed in the CUI Registry as a Specified Authority, then you must mark the CUI based on that Authority as CUI Specified and include that marking in the CUI Banner.

The CUI Registry may be found at https://www.archives.gov/cui/registry/category-list

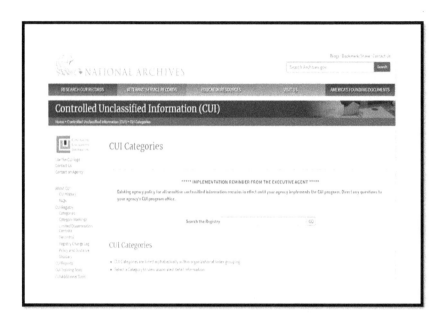

Banner Markings for Category and Subcategory Markings (Reference 32 CFR 2002.20(b)(2))

CUI Category or Subcategory Markings are separated by a double forward-slash (//) from the CUI Control Marking. When including multiple CUI Category or Subcategory Markings in the CUI Banner Marking, they must be separated by a single forward-slash (/). When a document contains CUI Specified, all CUI Specified Category or Subcategory Markings must be included in the CUI Banner Marking.

Additionally, agency heads may approve the use of CUI Basic Category or Subcategory Markings through agency CUI policy. When such agency policy exists, all CUI Basic Category or Subcategory Markings must be included in the CUI Banner Marking.

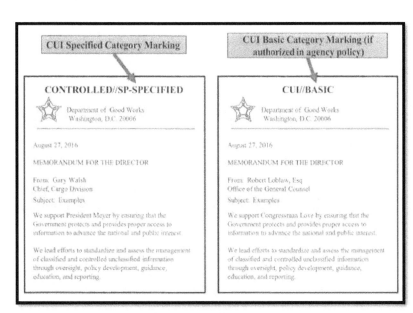

Varied Banner Markings

The above examples use the words "SP-SPECIFIED" and "BASIC" as substitutes for CUI Category and Subcategory Markings. Consult the CUI Registry for actual CUI markings.

Since CUI Specified Categories and Subcategories are different – both from CUI Basic and also from each other – CUI Specified MUST always be included in the CUI Banner. This is done to ensure that every authorized CUI holder and end-user who receives a document containing CUI Specified knows that the document must be treated in a manner that differs from CUI Basic. This is accomplished in two ways:

1. All CUI Specified documents must include the Category or Subcategory marking for all of the CUI Specified contained in that document in the CUI Banner Marking. This ensures that initially a user in receipt of that document is aware of the CUI Banner. This permits the user to be aware of whether they have something other than ordinary CUI Basic. It also allows the user to meet any additional or alternative requirements for the CUI Specified they hold.

2. To ensure that it is evident that a Category or Subcategory is Specified, the marking has "SP-" added to the beginning of the marking after the CUI or Controlled designation.

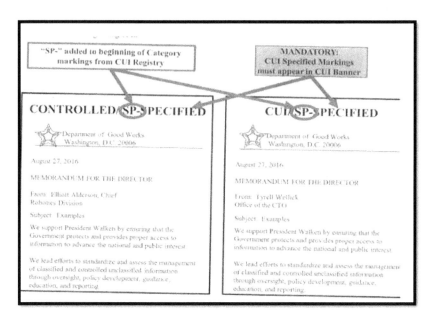

The above examples use the word "SPECIFIED" as a substitute for CUI Category and Subcategory Markings. Consult the CUI Registry for actual CUI markings.

Banner Markings with Multiple of Subcategory Markings (Reference 32 CFR 2002.20)

CUI Specified Markings must precede CUI Basic Markings where authorized for use by the agency head in the CUI Banner. Consult the agency CUI policy for guidance on the use of CUI Basic Category or Subcategory Markings. Additionally, CUI Category and Subcategory Markings MUST be alphabetized within CUI type (Basic or Specified).

Alphabetized Specified CUI categories and subcategories must precede alphabetized Basic CUI categories and subcategories.

Below are examples of CUI Banner Markings used in a document that contains both CUI Specified and CUI Basic.

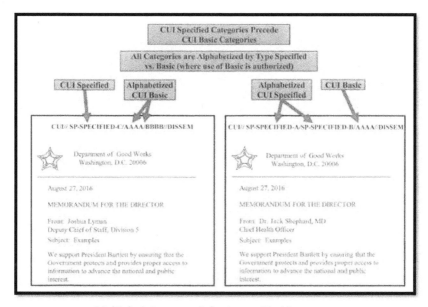

Multiple Category or Subcategory Markings

The above examples use "AAAA" and "BBBB" as substitutes for CUI Basic Category and Subcategory Markings, "SP-SPECIFIED-X" as a substitute for a CUI Specified Category and Subcategory Markings, and "DISSEM" as a substitute for a Limited Dissemination Control Marking. Consult the CUI Registry for actual CUI markings.

Banner Markings (Limited Dissemination Controls)(Reference 32 CFR 2002.20(b)(3)

Only Limited Dissemination (LIMDIS) Control Markings found in the CUI Registry are authorized for use with CUI. Limited Dissemination Control Markings are separated from preceding sections of the CUI Banner Marking by, double forward-slash *(///)*. When a document contains multiple Limited Dissemination Control Markings, those Limited Dissemination Control Markings MUST be alphabetized and separated from each other with a single forward-slash (/).

Below are examples that show the proper use of Limited Dissemination Control Markings in the CUI Banner Marking in a letter-type document or a slide presentation.

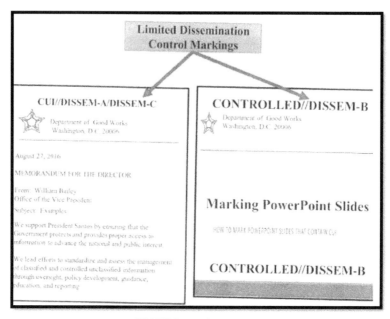

LIMDIS Controls

The above example uses "DISSEM-X" as a substitute for Limited Dissemination Control Markings. Consult the CUI Registry for actual CUI markings.

Designation Indicator (Reference 32 CFR 2002.20(a)(3)(d))

All documents containing CUI must indicate the designator's agency. This may be accomplished with letterhead, a signature block with the agency, or the use of a "Controlled by" line. Every effort should be made to identify a point of contact, branch, or division within an organization responsible for either the creation or protection of the CUI.

Below are examples of Designation Indicators in a slide presentation and a letter-type document.

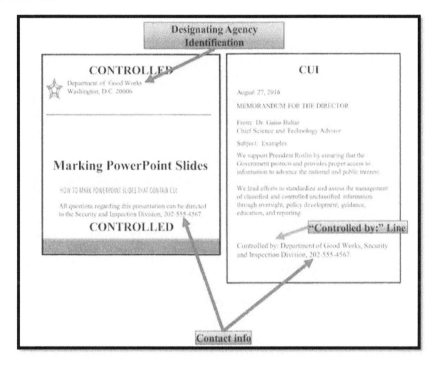

Designation Indicators

Portion Markings (Reference 32 CFR 2002.20(f))

Portion marking of CUI is *optional* in a fully unclassified document but is highly encouraged[22] to facilitate information sharing and proper handling of the information.

---

[22] The author strongly supports the use of portion markings. They further help when providing reports and responding to requests for information from the public; this provides clear boundaries for information release in accordance with the law.

Agency heads may approve the required use of CUI Portion marking on all CUI generated within their agency. Users should always consult their agency CUI policy when creating CUI documents.

When CUI Portion Marking is used, these rules will be followed. CUI Portion Markings are placed at the beginning of the portion (e.g., beginning of sentence or segment of the CUI), apply it throughout the entire document. CUI Portion Markings are contained within parentheses and may include up to three elements:

1. The CUI Control Marking: This is mandatory when portion marking and must be the acronym "CUI" (the word "Controlled" will not be used in portion marking).

2. CUI Category or Subcategory Markings: These can be found in the CUI Registry.

   a. When used, CUI Category or Subcategory Markings are separated from the CUI Control Marking by a double forward-slash(//).

   b. When including multiple categories or subcategories in a portion, CUI Category or Subcategory Markings are separated from each other by a single forward-slash (/).

3. Limited Dissemination Control Markings: These can be found in the CUI Registry and are separated from preceding CUI markings by a double forward-slash (//). When including multiple Limited Dissemination Control Markings, they must be alphabetized and separated from each other by a single forward-slash (/).

4. When CUI Portion Markings are used, and a portion does not contain CUI, a "U" is placed in parentheses to indicate that the portion contains Uncontrolled Unclassified Information.

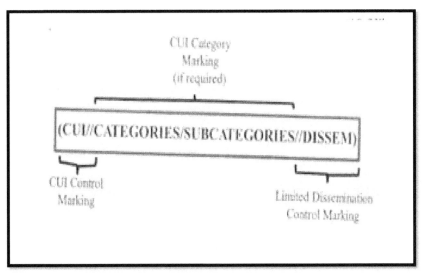

Portion Marking Standards

The above example uses the words "CATEGORIES" and "SUBCATEGORIES" as substitutes for CUI Category or Subcategory Markings and the word "DISSEM" as a substitute for a Limited Dissemination Control Marking. Consult the CUI Registry for actual CUI markings.

The presence of at least one item categorized as CUI in a document requires CUI marking of the entire document. CUI Portion Markings can be of significant assistance in determining if a document contains CUI and therefore must be marked appropriately. Additionally, when portion markings are used, and any portion does not contain CUI, a "(U)" is placed in front of that portion to indicate that it contains Uncontrolled or non-CUI - Unclassified[23] Information.

---

[23] Uncontrolled appears to be an ambiguous stamen from NARA; it is best considered as UNCLASSIFIED information that can be freely shared with the general public.

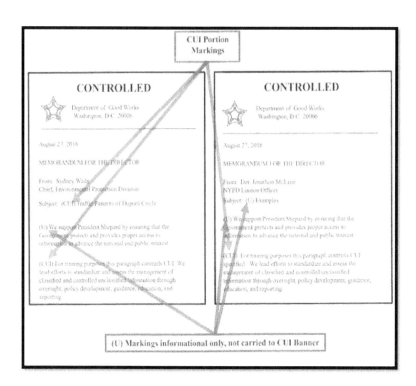

"Parenthetical" Portion Marking Examples

Portion Markings with Category Only (Reference 32 CFR 2002.20(f))

This example shows how to portion mark a document using the CUI Control Marking and CUI Category or Subcategory Markings. When a document contains CUI Specified, all CUI Specified Category or Subcategory Markings must be included in the CUI Banner Marking. Consult your agency CUI policy for guidance on the use of CUI Basic Category or Subcategory Markings. When CUI Portion Markings are used, and a portion does not contain CUI, a "U" is placed in parentheses to indicate that the portion contains Uncontrolled-Unclassified Information.

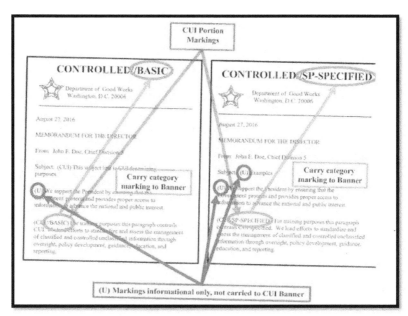

Portion Marking with Category Only

The above example uses "BASIC" and "SPECIFIED" as substitutes for CUI Category or Subcategory Markings. Consult the CUI Registry for actual CUI markings.

Portion Markings with Category and Dissemination Caveats (Reference 32 CFR 2002.20(f))

The example below shows how to portion mark a document using all three components of the CUI Banner Marking. When a document contains CUI Specified, CUI Specified Category or Subcategory Markings must be included in the CUI Banner Marking. Consult your agency CUI policy for guidance on the use of CUI Basic Category or Subcategory Markings. Also, when CUI Portion Markings are used, and a portion does not contain CUI, a "U" is placed in parentheses to indicate that the portion contains Uncontrolled-Unclassified Information.

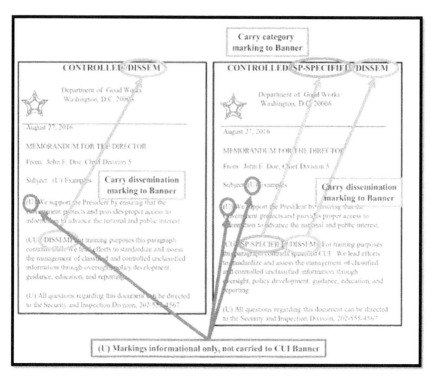

Portion Markings with Category and Dissemination

The above example uses "SP-SPECIFIED" as a substitute for a CUI Category or Subcategory Marking and "DISSEM" as a substitute for Limited Dissemination Control Markings. Consult the CUI Registry for actual CUI markings.

Common Mistakes in Banner Markings

Category and Subcategory Markings for CUI Specified MUST always be included in the Banner Marking, and those for CUI Basic may be required by agency CUI policy. When CUI Portion Markings are used and include CUI Category or Subcategory Markings, those markings MUST be included in the CUI Banner Marking.

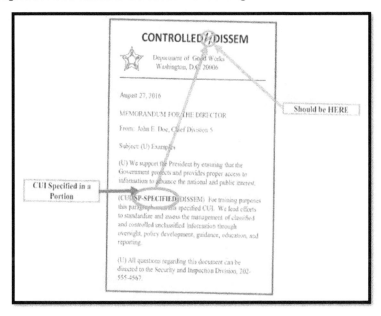

The above example uses "SP-SPECIFIED" as a substitute for a CUI Specified Category or Subcategory Marking and "DISSEM" as a substitute for a Limited Dissemination Control Marking. Consult the CUI Registry for actual CUI markings.

Marking of Multiple Pages (Reference 32 CFR 2002.20(c))

The composition of the CUI Banner Marking for a multi-page document is essentially the totality of all the CUI markings in the document; if any portion of the document contains CUI Specified or a Limited Dissemination Control Marking, then the CUI Banner Marking must reflect that.

Below is an example of one multi-page document with CUI Portion Marking.

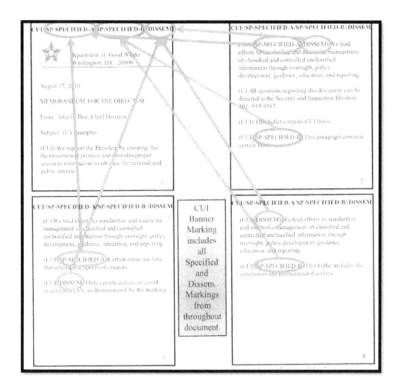

The overall CUI Banner Marking for the document must appear on all pages of the document.

Required Indicators as directed by Authorities (Reference 32 CFR 2002.20 (b)(2)(iii))

Required indicators that include informational, warning or dissemination statements may be mandated by the law, Federal regulation, or Government-wide policy that makes a specific item of information CUI. These indicators shall not be included in the CUI Banner or portion markings but must appear in a manner readily apparent to authorized personnel. This shall be consistent with the requirements of the governing document.

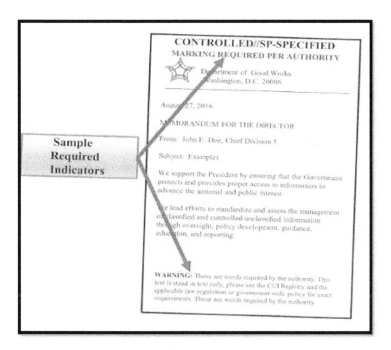

The above example uses "SPECIFIED" as a substitute for a CUI Specified Category or Subcategory Marking. Consult the CUI Registry for actual CUI markings.

Supplemental Administrative Markings (Reference 32 CFR 2002.20(l))

Agencies may use supplemental administrative markings (e.g., Draft, Deliberative, Pre- decisional, Provisional) along with CUI to inform recipients of the non-final status of documents ONLY when such markings are created and defined in agency policy.

Supplemental administrative markings may not be used to control CUI and may not be commingled with or incorporated into the CUI Banner Marking or Portion Markings. Supplemental administrative markings may not duplicate any marking in the CUI Registry.

Below are two examples of ways to properly use supplemental administrative markings.

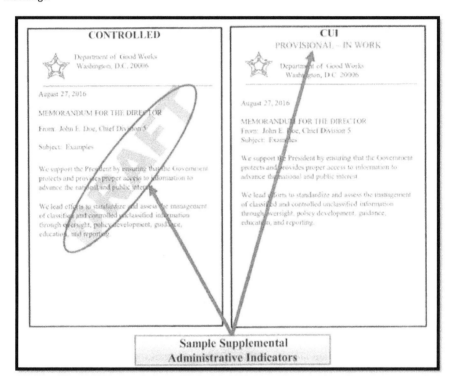

Common Mistakes for Supplemental Administrative Markings

Supplemental administrative markings may not be used to control CUI and must not be incorporated into CUI Banner Markings or CUI Portion Markings or duplicate any marking in the CUI Registry.

Below are two examples of ways **NOT** to use administrative markings.

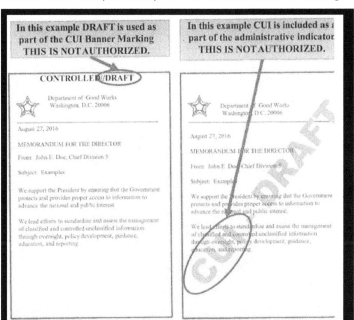

Electronic Media Storage and Marking Procedures (Reference 32 CFR 2002.20)

Media such as USB sticks, hard drives, and CD ROMs must be marked to alert CUI holders to the presence of CUI stored on the device. Due to space limitations, it may not be possible to include Category, Subcategory, or Limited Dissemination Control Markings on the given surface. At a minimum, mark media with the CUI Control Marking ("CONTROLLED" or "CUI") and the Designating Agency. Equipment can be marked or labeled to indicate that CUI is stored on the device.

Removable Hard drive

Equipment can be marked or labeled to indicate that CUI is stored on the device.

NOTE: DOGW is an acronym for Department of Good Works.

Marking Forms (Reference 32 CFR 2002.20)

Forms that contain CUI must be marked accordingly when completed. If space on the form is limited, cover sheets can be used for this purpose. As forms are updated during agency implementation of the CUI Program, they should be modified to include a statement that indicates the form is CUI when finalized.

CUI Control Marking

CONTROLLED
when filled in

Standard Form 86
Revised December 2010
U.S. Office of Personnel Management
5 CFR Parts 731, 732, and 736

QUESTIONNAIRE FOR
NATIONAL SECURITY POSITIONS

Form Approved
OMB No. 3206-0005

PERSONS COMPLETING THIS FORM SHOULD BEGIN WITH THE QUESTIONS BELOW AFTER CAREFULLY READING THE PRECEDING INSTRUCTIONS.

I have read the instructions and I understand that if I withhold, misrepresent, or falsify information on this form, I am subject to the penalties for inaccurate or false statement (per U. S. Criminal Code, Title 18, section 1001), denial or revocation of a security clearance, and/or removal and debarment from Federal Service.   ☐ YES   ☐ NO

Section 1 - Full Name
Provide your full name. If you have only initials in your name, provide them and indicate "Initial only". If you do not have a middle name, indicate "No Middle Name". If you are a "Jr.," "Sr.," etc. enter this under Suffix.

Last name	First name	Middle name	Suffix
BAUER	JACK	ALLEN	Sr

Section 2 - Date of Birth
Provide your date of birth (Month/Day/Year)
06/25/1969

Section 3 - Place of Birth
Provide your place of birth.

City	County	State	Country (Required)
ANYWHERE	THIS COUNTY	AK	United States

Section 4 - Social Security Number
Provide your U.S. Social Security Number.
123-45-6789   ☐ Not applicable

Section 5 - Other Names Used
Have you used any other names?   ☐ YES   ☒ NO (If NO, proceed to Section 6)

Complete the following if you have responded "Yes" to having used other names.
Provide your other name(s) used and the period of time you used it/them (for example: your maiden name(s), name(s) by a former marriage, former name(s), alias(es), or nicknames(s)). If you have only initials in your name(s), provide them and indicate "Initial only." If you do not have a middle name (s), indicate "No Middle Name" (NMN). If you are a "Jr.," "Sr.," etc. enter this under Suffix.

#1 Last name	First name	Middle name	Suffix

From (Month/Year)	To (Month/Year)	☐ Present	Maiden name?	Provide the reason(s) why the name changed

CUI Coversheets (Reference 32 CFR 2002.32)

The use of CUI coversheets is optional except when required by agency policy. Agencies may download coversheets from the CUI Registry or obtain printed copies through the General Services Administration (GSA) Global Supply Centers or the GSAAdvantage online service (https://www.gsa.gov/buying-selling/purchasing-programs/requisition-programs/gsa-global-supply/easy-ordering/gsa-global-supply-online-ordering).

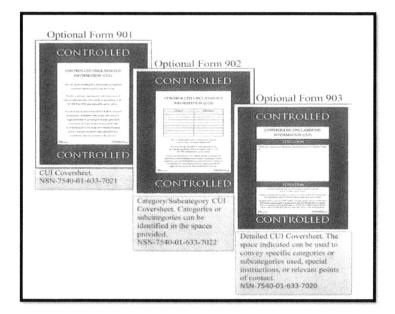

Marking Transmittal Documents (Reference 32 CFR 2002.20)

When a transmittal document accompanies CUI, the transmittal document must indicate that CUI is attached or enclosed. The transmittal document must also include, conspicuously, the following or similar instructions, as appropriate:

- "When the enclosure is removed, this document is Uncontrolled-Unclassified Information"; or

- "When the enclosure is removed, this document is (CUI Control Level); or

- "Upon removal, this document does not contain CUI."

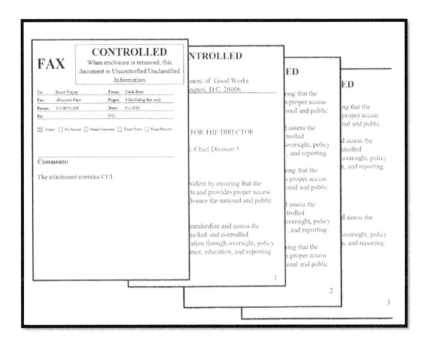

Alternate Marking Methods (Reference 32 CFR 2002.20)

Agency heads[24] may authorize the use of alternate marking methods on IT systems, websites, browsers, or databases through agency CUI policy. These may be used to alert users to the presence of CUI where the agency head has issued a limited CUI marking waiver for CUI designated within the agency. These warnings may take multiple forms and include the examples below.

---

[24] Agency Heads may be considered federal agency secretaries, leadership, etc., designated under contract to provide direct oversight of the agencies' CUI program.

Computer Monitor CUI Banners

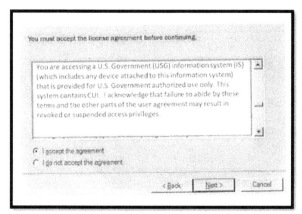

Agency or Company Legal Warning Notification

Room or Area Markings (Reference 32 CFR 2002.20)

In areas containing CUI, it may be necessary to alert personnel who are not authorized to access the area or information. This may be accomplished by any means approved by the agency and detailed in the agency's CUI policy. Typically, signs are posted exterior to the room or rooms, on all entry doors, and in any ante-room designated to verify clearances or need-to-know status of a group or individual.

Below is a sample of a sign that indicates CUI is present.

Example Exterior Door and Interior Rooms Sign

Container Markings (Reference 32 CFR 2002.20)

When an agency is storing CUI, authorized holders should mark the container to indicate that it contains CUI.

Below are some basic examples.

Shipping and Mailing (Reference 32 CFR 2002.20)

Agency heads must ensure that mailroom staffs are trained in handling CUI to include reporting any loss, theft, or misuse.

When shipping CUI:

- Address packages that contain CUI for delivery only to a specific recipient.

- DO NOT put CUI markings on the outside of an envelope or package for mailing/shipping.

- Use in-transit automated tracking and accountability tools where possible.

Re-marking Legacy Information (Reference 32 CFR 2002.36)

Legacy information is unclassified information that was marked as restricted from access or dissemination in some way or otherwise controlled before the CUI Program was established. **All legacy information is not automatically CUI.** Agencies must examine and determine what legacy information qualifies as CUI and mark it accordingly.

In cases of excessive burden, an agency's' head may issue a "Legacy Marking Waiver," as described in 32 CFR 2002.38(b) of the CUI Rule. When the agency head grants such a waiver, legacy material that qualifies need not be re-marked as CUI until and unless it is to be "re-used" in a new document.

LEGACY MARKING

Department of Good Works
Washington, D.C. 20006

August 27, 2016

MEMORANDUM FOR THE DIRECTOR

From: John E. Doe, Chief Division 5

Subject: Examples

We support the President by ensuring that the Government protects and provides proper access to information to advance the national and public interest.

We lead efforts to standardize and assess the management of classified and controlled unclassified information through oversight, policy development, guidance, education, and reporting.

"LEGACY MARKING" is used as a substitute for ad hoc, agency markings used to label unclassified information before the creation of the CUI Program.

When legacy information is to be re-used and incorporated into another document of any kind, it must undergo the process described below.

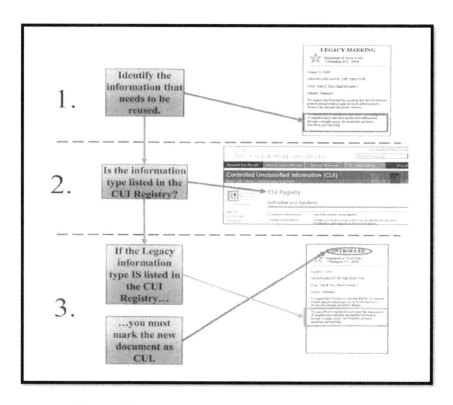

When possible contact the originator of the information for guidance in remarking and protecting the legacy information in the CUI Program.

CUI MARKINGS IN A CLASSIFIED ENVIRONMENT

Marking Commingled Information (Reference 32 CFR 2002.20(g))

When CUI is included in a document that contains any classified information, that document is referred to as **commingled**. Commingled documents are subject to the requirements of the CUI and Classified National Security Information (CNSI) Programs. As a best practice, keep the CUI and classified information in separate and designated areas to the greatest extent possible[25]. Mark all portions to ensure that authorized holders can distinguish CUI portions from those containing CNSI or Uncontrolled-Unclassified Information; the de-controlling provisions for CUI apply only to portions marked as CUI. CNSI portions remain classified to their declassification requirements.

Executive Order 13526 - Classified National Security Information

In the overall marking banner's CUI section, double forward slashes (//) are used to separate significant elements, and single forward slashes (/) are used to separate sub-

---

[25] Typically, classified facilities should be partitioned to include designated drawers, safes, and folders specific to CUI storage.

elements. The CUI Control Marking ("CUI") appears in the overall banner marking directly before the CUI category and subcategory markings. When there is CUI Specified in the document, CUI Specified category and subcategory marking(s) must appear in the overall banner marking. Per agency policy, if used, the optional CUI Basic category and subcategory markings would appear next. Both CUI Specified and CUI Basic markings are separately alphabetized. The limited dissemination control markings apply to the entire document and the CUI and classified information in it. Placeholders are not used for missing elements or sub-elements.

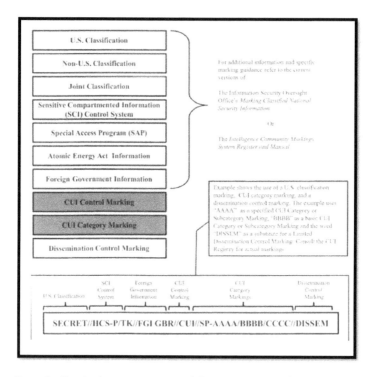

Commingling in the same paragraph is not recommended, where paragraphs contain CUI and CNSI commingled, portion marking elements follow a similar syntax to the banner marking. However, the paragraph

always takes the HIGHEST classification of the information contained in the paragraph.

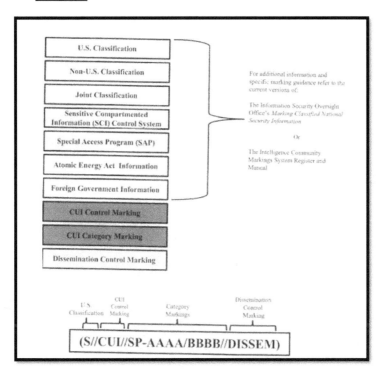

For additional information and specific marking, the guidance refers to the current versions of The Information Security Oversight Office's *Marking Classified National Security Information.*

Commingling Example 1

In cases where· CUI is commingled with classified information, the following applies:

- In banners, the CUI Control Marking is used only in its abbreviated form ("CUI"). The longer form ("CONTROLLED") is not used. Either the classification marking, CUI control marking ("CUI"), or the Uncontrolled Unclassified Marking ("U") must be used in every portion.

- Limited Dissemination Control Markings must appear in the banner line and in all portions to which they apply.

Best practice: CUI and CNSI should be placed in separate portions

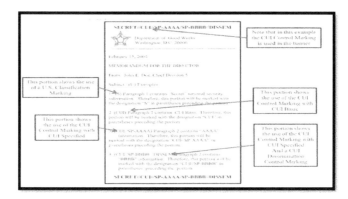

The above examples use "SP-AAAA" or "SP-BBBB" as CUI Specified Category or Subcategory Markings and the word "DISSEM" as a substitute for a Limited Dissemination Control Marking. Consult the CUI Registry for actual markings.

Commingling Example 2

These examples show the various ways CUI may be identified in a document.

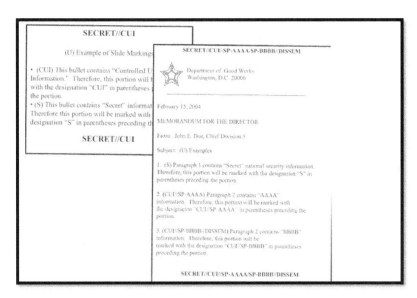

The above examples use "SP-AAAA" or "SP-BBBB" as CUI Specified Category or Subcategory Markings and the word "DISSEM" as a substitute for a Limited Dissemination Control Marking. Consult the CU Registry for actual markings.

Commingling Example 3

Below are two samples of CUI commingled with classified information, specifically with Classified National Security Information (CNSI). The sample on the left has the CUI and CNSI broken into separate paragraphs allowing for more natural future separation when needed to accommodate differing access requirements. The sample on the right has CUI and CNSI in the same paragraph.

The above examples use the word "SP-AAAA" as a substitute for a CUI Specified Category or Subcategory Marking. Consult the CUI Registry for actual markings.

Commingling Portion Markings (Reference 32 CFR 2002.20(g))

In a commingled document, when a portion contains both CUI and classified information, the portion marking for the classified information must precede the CUI Portion Marking. When commingling CUI with classified information, the user should retain the CUI, and classified portions separate to the greatest extent possible to allow for maximum information sharing. Many of the intricate markings seen below can be avoided by following this simple practice. Below are some examples of how to mark portions containing CUI.

Portion Marking	Contents of Portions Marked Section – CUI ONLY IN PORTION
(CUI)	This section contains CUI Basic.
(CUI/AAAA)	This section contains CUI Basic (with optional category marking).
(CUI/SP-BBBB)	This section contains CUI Specified.
(CUI/SP-BBBB/SP-CCCC)	This section contains two CUI Specified Categories in alphabetical order.
(CUI/DISSEM)	This section contains CUI Basic with a Limited Dissemination Control Marking
(CUI/AAAA//DISSEM)	This section contains CUI Basic with a Limited Dissemination Control Marking
(CUI/SP-BBBB//DISSEM)	This section contains CUI Specified with a Limited Dissemination Control Marking.
Portion Marking	**Contents of Portions Marked Section – WITH COMMINGLED PORTIONS (NOT RECOMMENDED)**
(S//CUI)	This section contains Secret information and CUI Basic.
(S//CUI/AAAA)	This section contains Secret information and CUI Basic (with optional category marking).
(S//CUI/SP-BBBB)	This section contains Secret information and CUI Specified.
(S//CUI/SP-BBBB/SP-CCCC)	This section contains Secret information and contains two CUI Specified Categories in alphabetical order.
(S//CUI/SP-BBBB//DISSEM)	This section contains Secret information and CUI Specified with a Limited Dissemination Control Marking.

APPENDIX D – NIST 800-171 Compliance Checklist

The following compliance checklist is intended to provide a guide to conduct a "self-assessment" of the company's overall cybersecurity posture as required by NIST 800-171.

*Assessment Method: Refer to NIST 800-171A, *Assessing Security Requirements for Controlled Unclassified Information*, that describes types and means to self-validate the control. The three assessment methods are examined, interviewed, and tested.

Control #	Description	Assessment Method*	Document (e.g., SSP or Co. Procedure Guide)	Page #	Reviewed By	Validated By
Access Control (AC)						
3.1.1	*Limit information system access to authorized users, processes acting on behalf of authorized users, or devices (including other information systems)*					
3.1.1[a]	*Authorized users are identified.*					
3.1.1[b]	*Processes acting on behalf of authorized users are identified.*					
3.1.1[c]	*Devices (and other systems) authorized to connect to the system are identified.*					
3.1.1[d]	*System access is limited to authorized users.*					
3.1.1[e]	*System access is limited to processes acting on behalf of authorized users.*					
3.1.1[f]	*System access is limited to authorized devices (including other systems).*					
3.1.1[a]	*Authorized users are identified.*					
3.1.2	*Limit information system access to the types of transactions and functions that authorized users are permitted to execute*					
3.1.2[a]	*The types of transactions and functions that authorized users are permitted to execute are defined.*					

3.1.2[b]	*System access is limited to the defined types of transactions and functions for authorized users.*	
3.1.3	***Control the flow of CUI in accordance with approved authorizations***	
3.1.3[a]	*Information flow control policies are defined.*	
3.1.3[b]	*Methods and enforcement mechanisms for controlling the flow of CUI are defined.*	
3.1.3[c]	*Designated sources and destinations (e.g., networks, individuals, and devices) for CUI within the system and between interconnected systems are identified.*	
3.1.3[d]	*Authorizations for controlling the flow of CUI are defined.*	
3.1.3[e]	*Approved authorizations for controlling the flow of CUI are enforced.*	
3.1.4	**Separate the duties of individuals to reduce the risk of malevolent activity without collusion**	
3.1.4[a]	*The duties of individuals requiring separation are defined.*	
3.1.4[b]	*Responsibilities for duties that require separation are assigned to separate individuals.*	
3.1.4[c]	*Access privileges that enable individuals to exercise the duties that require separation are granted to separate individuals.*	
3.1.5	***Employ the principle of least privilege, including for specific security functions and privileged accounts***	
3.1.5[a]	*Privileged accounts are identified.*	
3.1.5[b]	*Access to privileged accounts is authorized in accordance with the principle of least privilege.*	
3.1.5[c]	*Security functions are identified.*	
3.1.5[d]	*Access to security functions is authorized in accordance with the principle of least privilege.*	
3.1.6	***Use non-privileged accounts or roles when accessing nonsecurity functions***	

3.1.6[a]	Nonsecurity functions are identified.	
3.1.6[b]	Users are required to use non-privileged accounts or roles when accessing nonsecurity functions.	
3.1.7	**Prevent non-privileged users from executing privileged functions and audit the execution of such functions**	
3.1.7[a]	Privileged functions are defined.	
3.1.7[b]	Non-privileged users are defined.	
3.1.7[c]	Non-privileged users are prevented from executing privileged functions.	
3.1.7[d]	The execution of privileged functions is captured in audit logs.	
3.1.8	**Limit unsuccessful logon attempts**	
3.1.8[a]	The means of limiting unsuccessful logon attempts is defined.	
3.1.8[b]	The defined means of limiting unsuccessful logon attempts is implemented.	
3.1.9	**Provide privacy and security notices consistent with applicable CUI rules**	
3.1.9[a]	Privacy and security notices required by CUI-specified rules are identified, consistent, and associated with the specific CUI category.	
3.1.9[b]	Privacy and security notices are displayed.	
3.1.10	**Use session lock with pattern-hiding displays to prevent access/viewing of data after period of inactivity**	
3.1.10[a]	The period of inactivity after which the system initiates a session lock is defined.	
3.1.10[b]	Access to the system and viewing of data is prevented by initiating a session lock after the defined period of inactivity.	
3.1.10[c]	Previously visible information is concealed via a pattern-hiding display after the defined period of inactivity.	
3.1.11	**Terminate (automatically) a user session after a defined condition**	

3.1.11[a]	*Conditions requiring a user session to terminate are defined.*
3.1.11[b]	*A user session is automatically terminated after any of the defined conditions occur.*

Control #	Description	Assessment Method*	Document (e.g., SSP or Co. Procedure Guide)	Page #	Reviewed By	Valida ted By
Access Control (AC)						
3.1.12	*Monitor and control remote access sessions*					
3.1.12[a]	*Remote access sessions are permitted.*					
3.1.12[b]	*The types of permitted remote access are identified.*					
3.1.12[c]	*Remote access sessions are controlled.*					
3.1.12[d]	*Remote access sessions are monitored.*					
3.1.13	*Employ cryptographic mechanisms to protect the confidentiality of remote access sessions*					
3.1.13[a]	*Cryptographic mechanisms to protect the confidentiality of remote access sessions are identified.*					
3.1.13[b]	*Cryptographic mechanisms to protect the confidentiality of remote access sessions are implemented.*					
3.1.14	*Route remote access via managed access control points*					
3.1.14[a]	*Managed access control points are identified and implemented.*					
3.1.14[b]	*Remote access is routed through managed network access control points.*					
3.1.15	*Authorize remote execution of privileged commands and remote access to security-relevant information*					
3.1.15[a]	*Privileged commands authorized for remote execution are identified.*					
3.1.15[b]	*Security-relevant information authorized to be accessed remotely is identified.*					
3.1.15[c]	*The execution of the identified privileged commands via remote access is authorized.*					
3.1.15[d]	*Access to the identified security-relevant information via remote access is authorized.*					

3.1.16	***Authorize wireless access prior to allowing such connections***	
3.1.16[a]	*Wireless access points are identified.*	
3.1.16[b]	*Wireless access is authorized prior to allowing such connections.*	
3.1.17	***Protect wireless access using authentication and encryption***	
3.1.17[a]	*Wireless access to the system is protected using authentication.*	
3.1.17[b]	*Wireless access to the system is protected using encryption.*	
3.1.18	***Control connection of mobile devices***	
3.1.18[a]	*Mobile devices that process, store, or transmit CUI are identified.*	
3.1.18[b]	*Mobile device connections are authorized.*	
3.1.18[c]	*Mobile device connections are monitored and logged.*	
3.1.19	***Encrypt CUI on mobile devices***	
3.1.19[a]	*Mobile devices and mobile computing platforms that process, store, or transmit CUI are identified.*	
3.1.19[b]	*Encryption is employed to protect CUI on identified mobile devices and mobile computing platforms.*	
3.1.20[a]	*Connections to external systems are identified.*	
3.1.20[b]	*The use of external systems is identified.*	
3.1.20[c]	*Connections to external systems are verified.*	
3.1.20[d]	*The use of external systems is verified.*	
3.1.20[e]	*Connections to external systems are controlled/limited.*	
3.1.20[f]	*The use of external systems is controlled/limited.*	
3.1.20[a]	*Connections to external systems are identified.*	
3.1.21	***Limit use of organizational portable storage devices on external systems***	
3.1.21[a]	*The use of portable storage devices containing CUI on external systems is identified and documented.*	

3.1.21[b]	*Limits on the use of portable storage devices containing CUI on external systems are defined.*	
3.1.21[c]	*The use of portable storage devices containing CUI on external systems is limited as defined.*	
3.1.22	***Control CUI posted or processed on publicly accessible systems***	
3.1.22[a]	*Individuals authorized to post or process information on publicly accessible systems are identified.*	
3.1.22[b]	*Procedures to ensure CUI is not posted or processed on publicly accessible systems are identified.*	
3.1.22[c]	*A review process is in place prior to posting of any content to publicly accessible systems.*	
3.1.22[d]	*Content on publicly accessible systems is reviewed to ensure that it does not include CUI.*	
3.1.22[e]	*Mechanisms are in place to remove and address improper posting of CUI.*	
3.1.22[a]	*Individuals authorized to post or process information on publicly accessible systems are identified.*	

Control #	Description	Assessment Method*	Document (e.g., SSP or Co. Procedure Guide)	Page #	Reviewed By	Validated By
Awareness & Training (AT)						
3.2.1	*Ensure that managers, systems administrators, and users of organizational information systems are made aware of the security risks associated with their activities and of the applicable policies, standards, and procedures related to the security of organizational information systems*					
3.2.1[a]	*Security risks associated with organizational activities involving CUI are identified.*					
3.2.1[b]	*Policies, standards, and procedures related to the security of the system are identified.*					
3.2.1[c]	*Managers, systems administrators, and users of the system are made aware of the security risks associated with their activities.*					
3.2.1[d]	*Managers, systems administrators, and users of the system are made aware of the applicable policies, standards, and procedures related to the security of the system.*					
3.2.2	*Ensure that organizational personnel are adequately trained to carry out their assigned information security-related duties and responsibilities*					
3.2.2[a]	*Information security-related duties, roles, and responsibilities are defined.*					
3.2.2[b]	*Information security-related duties, roles, and responsibilities are assigned to designated personnel.*					
3.2.2[c]	*Personnel are adequately trained to carry out their assigned information security-related duties, roles, and responsibilities.*					
3.2.3	*Provide security awareness training on recognizing and reporting*					

	potential indicators of insider threat
3.2.3[a]	*Potential indicators associated with insider threats are identified.*
3.2.3[b]	*Security awareness training on recognizing and reporting potential indicators of insider threat is provided to managers and employees.*

Control #	Description	Assessment Method*	Document (e.g., SSP or Co. Procedure Guide)	Page #	Reviewed By	Validated By
Audit & Accountability (AU)						
3.3.1	*Create, protect, and retain information system audit records to the extent needed to enable the monitoring, analysis, investigation, and reporting of unlawful, unauthorized, or inappropriate information system activity*					
3.3.1[a]	*Audit logs needed (i.e., event types to be logged) to enable the monitoring, analysis, investigation, and reporting of unlawful or unauthorized system activity are specified.*					
3.3.1[b]	*The content of audit records needed to support monitoring, analysis, investigation, and reporting of unlawful or unauthorized system activity is defined.*					
3.3.1[c]	*Audit records are created (generated).*					
3.3.1[d]	*Audit records, once created, contain the defined content.*					
3.3.1[e]	*Retention requirements for audit records are defined.*					
3.3.1[f]	*Audit records are retained as defined.*					
3.3.2	*Ensure that the actions of individual information system users can be uniquely traced to those users, so they can be held accountable for their actions*					
3.3.2[a]	*The content of the audit records needed to support the ability to uniquely trace users to their actions is defined.*					
3.3.2[b]	*Audit records, once created, contain the defined content.*					
3.3.3	*Review and update audited events*					
3.3.3[a]	*A process for determining when to review logged events is defined.*					

3.3.3[b]	*Event types being logged are reviewed in accordance with the defined review process.*	
3.3.3[c]	*Event types being logged are updated based on the review.*	
3.3.4	***Alert in the event of an audit process failure***	
3.3.4[a]	*Personnel or roles to be alerted in the event of an audit logging process failure are identified.*	
3.3.4[b]	*Types of audit logging process failures for which alert will be generated are defined.*	
3.3.4[c]	*Identified personnel or roles are alerted in the event of an audit logging process failure.*	
3.3.5	***Correlate audit review, analysis, and reporting processes for investigation and response to indications of inappropriate, suspicious, or unusual activity***	
3.3.5[a]	*Audit record review, analysis, and reporting processes for investigation and response to indications of unlawful, unauthorized, suspicious, or unusual activity are defined.*	
3.3.5[b]	*Defined audit record review, analysis, and reporting processes are correlated.*	
3.3.6	***Provide audit reduction and report generation to support on-demand analysis and reporting***	
3.3.6[a]	*An audit record reduction capability that supports on-demand analysis is provided.*	
3.3.6[b]	*A report generation capability that supports on-demand reporting is provided.*	
3.3.7	***Provide an information system capability that compares and synchronizes internal system clocks with an authoritative source to generate time stamps for audit records***	

3.3.7[a]	Internal system clocks are used to generate timestamps for audit records.	
3.3.7[b]	An authoritative source with which to compare and synchronize internal system clocks is specified.	
3.3.7[c]	Internal system clocks used to generate timestamps for audit records are compared to and synchronized with the specified authoritative time source.	
3.3.8	**Protect audit information and audit tools from unauthorized access, modification, and deletion**	
3.3.8[a]	Audit information is protected from unauthorized access.	
3.3.8[b]	Audit information is protected from unauthorized modification.	
3.3.8[c]	Audit information is protected from unauthorized deletion.	
3.3.8[d]	Audit logging tools are protected from unauthorized access.	
3.3.8[e]	Audit logging tools are protected from unauthorized modification.	
3.3.8[f]	Audit logging tools are protected from unauthorized deletion.	
3.3.9	**Limit management of audit functionality to a subset of privileged users**	
3.3.9[a]	A subset of privileged users granted access to manage audit logging functionality is defined.	
3.3.9[b]	Management of audit logging functionality is limited to the defined subset of privileged users.	

Control #	Description	Assessment Method*	Document (e.g., SSP or Co. Procedure Guide)	Page #	Reviewed By	Validated By
Configuration Management (CM)						
3.4.1	*Establish and maintain baseline configurations and inventories of organizational information systems (including hardware, software, firmware, and documentation) throughout the respective system development life cycles*					
3.4.1[a]	*A baseline configuration is established.*					
3.4.1[b]	*The baseline configuration includes hardware, software, firmware, and documentation.*					
3.4.1[c]	*The baseline configuration is maintained (reviewed and updated) throughout the system development life cycle.*					
3.4.1[d]	*A system inventory is established.*					
3.4.1[e]	*The system inventory includes hardware, software, firmware, and documentation.*					
3.4.1[f]	*The inventory is maintained (reviewed and updated) throughout the system development life cycle.*					
3.4.2	*Establish and enforce security configuration settings for information technology products employed in organizational information systems*					
3.4.2[a]	*Security configuration settings for information technology products employed in the system are established and included in the baseline configuration.*					
3.4.2[b]	*Security configuration settings for information technology products employed in the system are enforced.*					

3.4.3	Track, review, approve/disapprove, and audit changes to information systems
3.4.3[a]	Changes to the system are tracked.
3.4.3[b]	Changes to the system are reviewed.
3.4.3[c]	Changes to the system are approved or disapproved.
3.4.3[d]	Changes to the system are logged.
3.4.4	**Analyze the security impact of changes prior to implementation**
3.4.5	**Define, document, approve and enforce physical and logical access restrictions associated with changes to the information system**
3.4.5[a]	Physical access restrictions associated with changes to the system are defined.
3.4.5[b]	Physical access restrictions associated with changes to the system are documented.
3.4.5[c]	Physical access restrictions associated with changes to the system are approved.
3.4.5[d]	Physical access restrictions associated with changes to the system are enforced.
3.4.5[e]	Logical access restrictions associated with changes to the system are defined.
3.4.5[f]	Logical access restrictions associated with changes to the system are documented.
3.4.5[g]	Logical access restrictions associated with changes to the system are approved.
3.4.5[h]	Logical access restrictions associated with changes to the system are enforced.
3.4.6	**Employ the principle of least functionality by configuring the information system to provide only essential capabilities**

3.4.6[a]	*Essential system capabilities are defined based on the principle of least functionality.*	
3.4.6[b]	*The system is configured to provide only the defined essential capabilities.*	
3.4.7	**Restrict, disable, and prevent the use of nonessential programs, functions, ports, protocols, and services**	
3.4.7[a]	*Essential programs are defined.*	
3.4.7[b]	*The use of nonessential programs is defined.*	
3.4.7[c]	*The use of nonessential programs is restricted, disabled, or prevented as defined.*	
3.4.7[d]	*Essential functions are defined.*	
3.4.7[e]	*The use of nonessential functions is defined.*	
3.4.7[f]	*The use of nonessential functions is restricted, disabled, or prevented as defined.*	
3.4.7[g]	*Essential ports are defined.*	
3.4.7[h]	*The use of nonessential ports is defined.*	
3.4.7[i]	*The use of nonessential ports is restricted, disabled, or prevented as defined.*	
3.4.7[j]	*Essential protocols are defined.*	
3.4.7[k]	*The use of nonessential protocols is defined.*	
3.4.7[l]	*The use of nonessential protocols is restricted, disabled, or prevented as defined.*	
3.4.7[m]	*Essential services are defined.*	
3.4.7[n]	*The use of nonessential services is defined.*	
3.4.7[o]	*The use of nonessential services is restricted, disabled, or prevented as defined.*	
3.4.8	**Apply deny-by-exception (blacklist) policy to prevent the use of unauthorized software or deny all, permit-by-exception (whitelisting) policy to allow the execution of authorized software**	

3.4.8[a]	*A policy specifying whether whitelisting or blacklisting is to be implemented is specified.*	
3.4.8[b]	*The software allowed to execute under whitelisting or denied use under blacklisting is specified.*	
3.4.8[c]	*Whitelisting to allow the execution of authorized software or blacklisting to prevent the use of unauthorized software is implemented as specified.*	
3.4.9	***Control and monitor user-installed software***	
3.4.9[a]	*A policy for controlling the installation of software by users is established.*	
3.4.9[b]	*Installation of software by users is controlled based on the established policy.*	
3.4.9[c]	*Installation of software by users is monitored.*	

Control #	Description	Assessment Method*	Document (e.g., SSP or Co. Procedure Guide)	Page #	Reviewed By	Validated By
Identification & Authentication (IA)						
3.5.1	*Identify information system users, processes acting on behalf of users, or devices*					
3.5.1[a]	*System users are identified.*					
3.5.1[b]	*Processes acting on behalf of users are identified.*					
3.5.1[c]	*Devices accessing the system are identified.*					
3.5.2	*Authenticate (or verify) the identities of those users, processes, or devices, as a prerequisite to allowing access to organizational information systems*					
3.5.2[a]	*The identity of each user is authenticated or verified as a prerequisite to system access.*					
3.5.2[b]	*The identity of each process acting on behalf of a user is authenticated or verified as a prerequisite to system access.*					
3.5.2[c]	*The identity of each device accessing or connecting to the system is authenticated or verified as a prerequisite to system access.*					
3.5.3	*Use multifactor authentication for local and network access to privileged accounts and for network access to non-privileged accounts*					
3.5.3[a]	*Privileged accounts are identified.*					
3.5.3[b]	*Multifactor authentication is implemented for local access to privileged accounts.*					
3.5.3[c]	*Multifactor authentication is implemented for network access to privileged accounts.*					

3.5.3[d]	Multifactor authentication is implemented for network access to non-privileged accounts.	
3.5.4	**Employ replay-resistant authentication mechanisms for network access to privileged and nonprivileged accounts**	
3.5.5	**Prevent reuse of identifiers for a defined period**	
3.5.5[a]	A period within which identifiers cannot be reused is defined.	
3.5.5[b]	Reuse of identifiers is prevented within the defined period.	
3.5.6	**Disable identifiers after a defined period of inactivity**	
3.5.6[a]	A period of inactivity after which an identifier is disabled is defined.	
3.5.6[b]	Identifiers are disabled after the defined period of inactivity.	
3.5.7	**Enforce a minimum password complexity and change of characters when new passwords are created**	
3.5.7[a]	Password complexity requirements are defined.	
3.5.7[b]	Password change of character requirements is defined.	
3.5.7[c]	Minimum password complexity requirements, as defined, are enforced when new passwords are created.	
3.5.7[d]	Minimum password change of character requirements as defined is enforced when new passwords are created.	
3.5.8	**Prohibit password reuse for a specified number of generations**	
3.5.8[a]	The number of generations during which a password cannot be reused is specified.	
3.5.8[b]	Reuse of passwords is prohibited during the specified number of generations.	

3.5.9	Allow temporary password use for system logons with an immediate change to a permanent password	
3.5.10	Store and transmit only encrypted representation of passwords	
3.5.10[a]	Passwords are cryptographically protected in storage.	
3.5.10[b]	Passwords are cryptographically protected in transit.	
3.5.11.	Obscure feedback of authentication information	

Control #	Description	Assessment Method*	Document (e.g., SSP or Co. Procedure Guide)	Page #	Reviewed By	Validated By
Incident Response (IR)						
3.6.1	*Establish an operational incident-handling capability for organizational information systems that includes adequate preparation, detection, analysis, containment, recovery, and user response activities*					
3.6.1[a]	*An operational incident-handling capability is established.*					
3.6.1[b]	*The operational incident-handling capability includes preparation.*					
3.6.1[c]	*The operational incident-handling capability includes detection.*					
3.6.1[d]	*The operational incident-handling capability includes analysis.*					
3.6.1[e]	*The operational incident-handling capability includes containment.*					
3.6.1[f]	*The operational incident-handling capability includes recovery.*					
3.6.1[g]	*The operational incident-handling capability includes user response activities.*					
3.6.2	*Track, document, and report incidents to appropriate officials and/or authorities both internal and external to the organization*					
3.6.2[a]	*Incidents are tracked.*					
3.6.2[b]	*Incidents are documented.*					
3.6.2[c]	*Authorities to whom incidents are to be reported are identified.*					
3.6.2[d]	*Organizational officials to whom incidents are to be reported are identified.*					
3.6.2[e]	*Identified authorities are notified of incidents.*					

3.6.2[f]	*Identified organizational officials are notified of incidents.*	
3.6.3	***Test the organizational incident response capability***	

Control #	Description	Assessment Method*	Document (e.g., SSP or Co. Procedure Guide)	Page #	Reviewed By	Validated By
Maintenance (MA)						
3.7.1	*Perform maintenance on organizational information systems*					
3.7.2	*Provide effective controls on the tools, techniques, mechanisms, and personnel used to conduct information system maintenance*					
3.7.2[a]	*Tools used to conduct system maintenance are controlled.*					
3.7.2[b]	*Techniques used to conduct system maintenance are controlled.*					
3.7.2[c]	*Mechanisms used to conduct system maintenance are controlled.*					
3.7.2[d]	*Personnel used to conduct system maintenance are controlled.*					
3.7.3	**Ensure equipment removed for off-site maintenance is sanitized of any CUI**					
3.7.4	*Check media containing diagnostic and test programs for malicious code before the media are used in the information system*					
3.7.5	*Require multifactor authentication to establish nonlocal maintenance sessions via external network connections and terminate such connections when nonlocal maintenance is complete*					
3.7.5[a]	*Multifactor authentication is used to establish nonlocal maintenance sessions via external network connections.*					
3.7.5[b]	*Nonlocal maintenance sessions established via external network connections are terminated when nonlocal maintenance is complete.*					

3.7.6	*Supervise the maintenance activities of maintenance personnel without required access authorization*	

Control #	Description	Assessment Method*	Document (e.g., SSP or Co. Procedure Guide)	Page #	Reviewed By	Validated By
Media Protection (MP)						
3.8.1	**Protect (i.e., physically control and securely store) information system media containing CUI, both paper and digital**					
3.8.1[a]	Paper media containing CUI is physically controlled.					
3.8.1[b]	Digital media containing CUI is physically controlled.					
3.8.1[c]	Paper media containing CUI is securely stored.					
3.8.1[d]	Digital media containing CUI is securely stored.					
3.8.2	**Limit access to CUI on information system media to authorized users**					
3.8.3	**Sanitize or destroy information system media containing CUI before disposal or release for reuse**					
3.8.3[a]	System media containing CUI is sanitized or destroyed before disposal.					
3.8.3[b]	System media containing CUI is sanitized before it is released for reuse.					
3.8.4	**Mark media with necessary CUI markings and distribution limitations**					
3.8.4[a]	Media containing CUI is marked with applicable CUI markings.					
3.8.4[b]	Media containing CUI is marked with distribution limitations.					
3.8.5	**Control access to media containing CUI and maintain accountability for media during transport outside of controlled areas**					
3.8.5[a]	Access to media containing CUI is controlled.					

3.8.5[b]	*Accountability for media containing CUI is maintained during transport outside of controlled areas.*	
3.8.6	**Implement cryptographic mechanisms to protect the confidentiality of CUI stored on digital media during transport unless otherwise protected by alternative physical safeguards**	
3.8.7	**Control the use of removable media on information system components**	
3.8.8	**Prohibit the use of portable storage devices when such devices have no identifiable owner**	
3.8.9	**Protect the confidentiality of backup CUI at storage locations**	

Control #	Description	Assessment Method*	Document (e.g., SSP or Co. Procedure Guide)	Page #	Reviewed By	Validated By
Personnel Security (PS)						
3.9.1	*Screen individuals prior to authorizing access to information systems containing CUI*					
3.9.2	*Ensure that CUI and information systems containing CUI are protected during and after personnel actions such as terminations and transfers*					
3.9.2[a]	*A policy and/or process for terminating system access and any credentials coincident with personnel actions is established.*					
3.9.2[b]	*System access and credentials are terminated consistent with personnel actions such as termination or transfer.*					
3.9.2[c]	*The system is protected during and after personnel transfer actions.*					

Control #	Description	Assessment Method*	Document (e.g., SSP or Co. Procedure Guide)	Page #	Reviewed By	Validated By
Physical Security (PP)						
3.10.1	*Limit physical access to organizational information systems, equipment, and the respective operating environments to authorized individuals*					
3.10.1[a]	*Authorized individuals allowed physical access are identified.*					
3.10.1[b]	*Physical access to organizational systems is limited to authorized individuals.*					
3.10.1[c]	*Physical access to equipment is limited to authorized individuals.*					
3.10.1[d]	*Physical access to operating environments is limited to authorized individuals.*					
3.10.2	*Protect and monitor the physical facility and support infrastructure for those information systems*					
3.10.2[a]	*The physical facility where organizational systems reside is protected.*					
3.10.2[b]	*The support infrastructure for organizational systems is protected.*					
3.10.2[c]	*The physical facility where organizational systems reside is monitored.*					
3.10.2[d]	*The support infrastructure for organizational systems is monitored.*					
3.10.3	*Escort visitors and monitor visitor activity*					
3.10.3[a]	*Visitors are escorted.*					
3.10.3[b]	*Visitor activity is monitored.*					
3.10.4	*Maintain audit logs of physical access*					
3.10.5	*Control and manage physical access devices*					

3.10.5[a]	*Physical access devices are identified.*
3.10.5[b]	*Physical access devices are controlled.*
3.10.5[c]	*Physical access devices are managed.*
3.10.6	***Enforce safeguarding measures for CUI at alternate worksites (e.g., telework sites)***
3.10.6[a]	*Safeguarding measures for CUI are defined for alternate work sites.*
3.10.6[b]	*Safeguarding measures for CUI are enforced for alternate work sites.*

Control #	Description	Assessment Method*	Document (e.g., SSP or Co. Procedure Guide)	Page #	Reviewed By	Validated By
Risk Assessments (RA)						
3.11.1	*Periodically assess the risk to organizational operations (including mission, functions, image, or reputation), organizational assets, and individuals, resulting from the operation of organizational information systems and the associated processing, storage, or transmission of CUI*					
3.11.1[a]	*The frequency to assess the risk to organizational operations, organizational assets, and individuals are defined.*					
3.11.1[b]	*The risk to organizational operations, organizational assets, and individuals resulting from the operation of an organizational system that processes, stores, or transmits CUI is assessed with the defined frequency.*					
3.11.2	*Scan for vulnerabilities in the information system and applications periodically and when new vulnerabilities affecting the system are identified*					
3.11.2[a]	*The frequency to scan for vulnerabilities in organizational systems and applications is defined.*					
3.11.2[b]	*Vulnerability scans are performed on organizational systems with the defined frequency.*					
3.11.2[c]	*Vulnerability scans are performed on applications with the defined frequency.*					
3.11.2[d]	*Vulnerability scans are performed on organizational systems when new vulnerabilities are identified.*					

3.11.2[e]	Vulnerability scans are performed on applications when new vulnerabilities are identified.	
3.11.3	**Remediate vulnerabilities in accordance with assessments of risk**	
3.11.3[a]	Vulnerabilities are identified.	
3.11.3[b]	Vulnerabilities are remediated in accordance with risk assessments.	

Control #	Description	Assessment Method*	Document (e.g., SSP or Co. Procedure Guide)	Page #	Reviewed By	Validated By
Security Assessments (SA)						
3.12.1	**Periodically assess the security controls in organizational information systems to determine if the controls are effective in their application**					
3.12.1[a]	The frequency of security control assessments is defined.					
3.12.1[b]	Security controls are assessed with the defined frequency to determine if the controls are effective in their application.					
3.12.2	**Develop and implement plans of action designed to correct deficiencies and reduce or eliminate vulnerabilities in organizational information systems**					
3.12.2[a]	Deficiencies and vulnerabilities to be addressed by the plan of action are identified.					
3.12.2[b]	A plan of action is developed to correct identified deficiencies and reduce or eliminate identified vulnerabilities.					
3.12.2[c]	The plan of action is implemented to correct identified deficiencies and reduce or eliminate identified vulnerabilities.					
3.12.3	**Monitor information system security controls on an ongoing basis to ensure the continued effectiveness of the controls**					
3.12.4	**Develop, document, and periodically update system security plans that describe system boundaries, system environments of operation, how security requirements are implemented, and the**					

	relationships with or connections to other systems	
3.12.4[a]	*A system security plan is developed.*	
3.12.4[b]	*The system boundary is described and documented in the system security plan.*	
3.12.4[c]	*The system environment of operation is described and documented in the system security plan.*	
3.12.4[d]	*The security requirements identified and approved by the designated authority as non-applicable are identified.*	
3.12.4[e]	*The method of security requirement implementation is described and documented in the system security plan.*	
3.12.4[f]	*The relationship with or connection to other systems is described and documented in the system security plan.*	
3.12.4[g]	*The frequency to update the system security plan is defined.*	
3.12.4[h]	*System security plan is updated with the defined frequency.*	

Control #	Description	Assessment Method*	Document (e.g., SSP or Co. Procedure Guide)	Page #	Reviewed By	Validated By
System & Communications Protection (SC)						
3.13.1	*Monitor, control, and protect organizational communications (i.e., information transmitted or received by organizational information systems) at the external boundaries and key internal boundaries of the information systems*					
3.13.1[a]	*The external system boundary is defined.*					
3.13.1[b]	*Key internal system boundaries are defined.*					
3.13.1[c]	*Communications are monitored at the external system boundary.*					
3.13.1[d]	*Communications are monitored at key internal boundaries.*					
3.13.1[e]	*Communications are controlled at the external system boundary.*					
3.13.1[f]	*Communications are controlled at key internal boundaries.*					
3.13.1[g]	*Communications are protected at the external system boundary.*					
3.13.1[h]	*Communications are protected at key internal boundaries.*					
3.13.2	*Employ architectural designs, software development techniques, and systems engineering principles that promote effective information security within organizational information systems*					
3.13.2[a]	*Architectural designs that promote effective information security are identified.*					
3.13.2[b]	*Software development techniques that promote effective information security are identified.*					

3.13.2[c]	Systems engineering principles that promote effective information security are identified.	
3.13.2[d]	Identified architectural designs that promote effective information security are employed.	
3.13.2[e]	Identified software development techniques that promote effective information security are employed.	
3.13.2[f]	Identified systems engineering principles that promote effective information security are employed.	
3.13.3	**Separate user functionality from information system management functionality**	
3.13.3[a]	User functionality is identified.	
3.13.3[b]	System management functionality is identified.	
3.13.3[c]	User functionality is separated from system management functionality.	
3.13.4	**Prevent unauthorized and unintended information transfer via shared system resources**	
3.13.5	**Implement subnetworks for publicly accessible system components that are physically or logically separated from internal networks**	
3.13.5[a]	Publicly accessible system components are identified.	
3.13.5[b]	Subnetworks for publicly accessible system components are physically or logically separated from internal networks.	
3.13.6	**Deny network communications traffic by default and allow network communications traffic by exception (i.e., deny all, permit by exception)**	
3.13.6[a]	Network communications traffic is denied by default.	
3.13.6[b]	Network communications traffic is allowed by exception.	

| 3.13.7 | *Prevent remote devices from simultaneously establishing non-remote connections with the information system and communicating via some other connection to resources in external networks* |

Control #	Description	Assessment Method*	Document (e.g., SSP or Co. Procedure Guide)	Page #	Reviewed By	Valid ated By
System & Communications Protection (SC)						
3.13.8	*Implement cryptographic mechanisms to prevent unauthorized disclosure of CUI during transmission unless otherwise protected by alternative physical safeguards*					
3.13.8[a]	*Cryptographic mechanisms intended to prevent unauthorized disclosure of CUI are identified.*					
3.13.8[b]	*Alternative physical safeguards intended to prevent unauthorized disclosure of CUI are identified.*					
3.13.8[c]	*Either cryptographic mechanisms or alternative physical safeguards are implemented to prevent unauthorized disclosure of CUI during transmission.*					
3.13.9	*Terminate network connections associated with communications sessions at the end of the sessions or after a defined period of inactivity*					
3.13.9[a]	*A period of inactivity to terminate network connections associated with communications sessions is defined.*					
3.13.9[b]	*Network connections associated with communications sessions are terminated at the end of the sessions.*					
3.13.9[c]	*Network connections associated with communications sessions are terminated after the defined period of inactivity.*					
3.13.10	*Establish and manage cryptographic keys for cryptography employed in the information system*					
3.13.10[a]	*Cryptographic keys are established whenever cryptography is employed.*					
3.13.10[b]	*Cryptographic keys are managed whenever cryptography is employed.*					

3.13.11	***Employ FIPS-validated cryptography when used to protect the confidentiality of CUI***	
3.13.12	***Prohibit remote activation of collaborative computing devices and provide indication of devices in use to users present at the device***	
3.13.12[a]	Collaborative computing devices are identified.	
3.13.12[b]	Collaborative computing devices provide indication to users of devices in use.	
3.13.12[c]	Remote activation of collaborative computing devices is prohibited.	
3.13.13	***Control and monitor the use of mobile code***	
3.13.13[a]	Use of mobile code is controlled.	
3.13.13[b]	Use of mobile code is monitored.	
3.13.14	***Control and monitor the use of Voice over Internet Protocol (VoIP) technologies***	
3.13.14[a]	Use of Voice over Internet Protocol (VoIP) technologies is controlled.	
3.13.14[b]	Use of Voice over Internet Protocol (VoIP) technologies is monitored.	
3.13.15	***Protect the authenticity of communications sessions***	
3.13.16	***Protect the confidentiality of CUI at rest***	

Control #	Description	Assessment Method*	Document	Page #	Reviewed By	Validated By
System & Information Integrity (SI)						
3.14.1	*Identify, report, and correct information and information system flaws in a timely manner*					
3.14.1[a]	*The time within which to identify system flaws is specified.*					
3.14.1[b]	*System flaws are identified within the specified time frame.*					
3.14.1[c]	*The time within which to report system flaws is specified.*					
3.14.1[d]	*System flaws are reported within the specified time frame.*					
3.14.1[e]	*The time within which to correct system flaws is specified.*					
3.14.1[f]	*System flaws are corrected within the specified time frame.*					
3.14.2	*Provide protection from malicious code at appropriate locations within organizational information systems*					
3.14.2[a]	*Designated locations for malicious code protection are identified.*					
3.14.2[b]	*Protection from malicious code at designated locations is provided.*					
3.14.3	*Monitor information system security alerts and advisories and take appropriate actions in response*					
3.14.3[a]	*Response actions to system security alerts and advisories are identified.*					
3.14.3[b]	*System security alerts and advisories are monitored.*					
3.14.3[c]	*Actions in response to system security alerts and advisories are taken.*					
3.14.4	*Update malicious code protection mechanisms when new releases are available*					
3.14.5	*Perform periodic scans of the information system and real-*					

	time scans of files from external sources as files are downloaded, opened, or executed	
3.14.5[a]	*The frequency for malicious code scans is defined.*	
3.14.5[b]	*Malicious code scans are performed with the defined frequency.*	
3.14.5[c]	*Real-time malicious code scans of files from external sources as files are downloaded, opened, or executed are performed.*	
3.14.6	**Monitor the information system including inbound and outbound communications traffic, to detect attacks and indicators of potential attacks**	
3.14.6[a]	*The system is monitored to detect attacks and indicators of potential attacks.*	
3.14.6[b]	*Inbound communications traffic is monitored to detect attacks and indicators of potential attacks.*	
3.14.6[c]	*Outbound communications traffic is monitored to detect attacks and indicators of potential attacks.*	
3.14.7	**Identify unauthorized use of the information system**	
3.14.7[a]	*Authorized use of the system is defined.*	
3.14.7[b]	*Unauthorized use of the system is identified.*	

About the Author

Mr. Russo is a former Senior Information Security Engineer with the Department of Defense's (DOD) F-35 Joint Strike Fighter program. He has an extensive background in cybersecurity and is an expert in the Risk Management Framework (RMF) and DOD Instruction 8510 which implements RMF throughout the DOD and the federal government. He holds both a Certified Information Systems Security Professional (CISSP) certification and a CISSP in information security architecture (ISSAP). He holds a 2017 certification as a Chief Information Security Officer (CISO) from the National Defense University, Washington, DC. He retired from the US Army Reserves in 2012 as the Senior Intelligence Officer.

He is the former CISO at the Department of Education. During his tenure, he led an aggressive effort to close over 95% of the outstanding US Congressional and Inspector General cybersecurity shortfall weaknesses spanning as far back as five years. He regularly speaks within the federal government and Intelligence Community on advanced topics regarding the evolution of cybersecurity in the 21st Century.

Mr. Russo is the former Senior Cybersecurity Engineer supporting the Joint Medical Logistics Development Functional Center of the Defense Health Agency (DHA) at Fort Detrick, MD. He led a team of engineering and cybersecurity professionals protecting five major Medical Logistics systems supporting over 200 DOD Medical Treatment Facilities around the globe.

In 2011, Mr. Russo was certified by the Office of Personnel Management as a graduate of the Senior Executive Service Candidate program.

From 2009 through 2011, Mr. Russo was the Chief Technology Officer at the Small Business Administration (SBA). He led a team of over 100 IT professionals in supporting an intercontinental Enterprise IT infrastructure and security operations spanning 12-time zones; he deployed cutting-edge technologies to enhance SBA's business and information sharing operations supporting the small business community. Mr. Russo was the first-ever Program Executive Officer (PEO)/Senior Program Manager in the Office of Intelligence & Analysis at Headquarters, Department of Homeland Security (DHS), Washington, DC. Mr. Russo was responsible for the development and deployment of secure Information and Intelligence support systems for OI&A to include software applications and systems to enhance the DHS mission. He was responsible for the program management development lifecycle during his tenure at DHS.

He holds a Master of Science from the National Defense University in Government Information Leadership with a concentration in Cybersecurity and a Bachelor of Arts in Political Science with a minor in Russian Studies from Lehigh University. He holds Level III Defense Acquisition certification in Program Management, Information Technology, and Systems Engineering. He has been a member of the DOD Acquisition Corps since 2001.

Writing an Effective Plan of Action & Milestones (POAM): ~ 2nd Edition: Universal Version

WHAT IS A PLAN OF ACTION AND MILESTONES (POAM)?

A POAM is precisely what it is as described. It is a plan, specific to the selected security controls that cannot be adequately addressed, or a vulnerability identified by security tools that assess the cybersecurity posture of an Information System (IS), and the associated plan to fix it. It is typically applied to the local physical and virtual network infrastructure that provides the "backbone" processes for a company to conduct business. Further, a POAM requires milestones. These are benchmark points in time that a company is expected to work to move a non-compliant control to a compliant status. Milestones are interim efforts that are managed by the IT staff and with corporate officer oversight to ensure an active risk management effort occurs. This Second Edition considers improved approaches and tools to manage the lifecycle of an active POAM.

NIST 800-171: System Security Plan (SSP) Template & Workbook: ~ SECOND EDITION

THE SYSTEM SECURITY PLAN IS A CRITICAL DOCUMENT FOR NIST 800-171, AND WE HAVE RELEASED A MORE EXPANSIVE AND UP TO DATE SECOND EDITION FOR 2019

The guidance here is also designed to support the growing challenges within the California Consumer Privacy Act (CCPA) and has wide-ranging applicability for any agency or business following the NIST 800-171 framework.

This is part of an ongoing series of Cybersecurity Self Help documents being developed to address the recent changes and requirements levied by the Federal Government on contractors wishing to do business with the government. The intent of these supplements is to provide immediate and valuable information, so business owners and their Information Technology (IT) staff need. The changes are coming rapidly for cybersecurity contract requirements. Are you ready? We plan to be ahead of the curve with you with high-quality books that can provide immediate support to the ever-growing challenges of cyber-threats to the Government and your business.

Downloadable versions of the SSP, POAM, and NIST 800-171 Compliance templates may be found at https://cybersentinel.tech on the "Cybershop" page.

www.ingramcontent.com/pod-product-compliance
Lightning Source LLC
LaVergne TN
LVHW081337050326
832903LV00024B/1182